COMMITTED TO CRAFTSMANSHIP

In Biblical Counseling

Jay E. Adams

Institute for Nouthetic Studies, a ministry of Mid-America Baptist Theological Seminary, 2095 Appling Road, Cordova, TN 38016
mabts.edu / nouthetic.org / INSBookstore.com

Committed to Craftsmanship in Biblical Counseling by Jay E. Adams
Copyright © 2019 by the Institute for Nouthetic Studies,
© 2000 by Jay E. Adams
New Testament quotations are from the *Christian Counselor's New Testament and Proverbs*
Copyright © 2019 by the Institute for Nouthetic Studies,
© 1977, 1980, 1994, 2000 by Jay E. Adams
Biblical quotations in the text are indicated by boldface type.

ISBN: 978-1-949737-00-4 (Print)
ISBN: 978-1-949737-01-1 (eBook)
Old ISBN: 978-1-889032-23-9

Editor: Donn R. Arms
Design: James Wendorf | www.FaithfulLifePublishers.com

Library of Congress Cataloging-in-Publication Data
Names: Adams, Jay E., 1929-
Title: *Committed to Craftsmanship in Biblical Counseling* / Jay E. Adams

Description: Cordova: Institute for Nouthetic Studies, 2019 Identifiers: LCCN 2018968517 | ISBN 9781949737004 (paper) Subjects: LCHS: Counseling – Religious Aspects – Christianity. Classification: LCC BV4012.2.A323 | DDC 253.5

All rights reserved. No part of this publication may be reproduced, stored in a retrieval system, or transmitted in any form or by any means – electronic, mechanical, photocopy, recording, or any other – except for brief quotations in printed reviews, without prior permission of the publisher.

Published in the United States of America

Preface to the Second Printing

I send forth this second edition of *Committed to Craftsmanship* with the hope that, distributed by a new publisher, it will find its way into the hands of many who did not know of its existence previously. My goal is to effect many who need to be challenged to work more faithfully and carefully for the Lord. If it is used to do so, I will be grateful. May He so use this volume!

— Jay E Adams

CONTENTS

Introduction 9
1. Why All the Fuss? 12
2. Committed to Craftsmanship 17
3. The Threat of Eclecticism 20
4. What Does a Biblical Counselor Do? 26
5. Beginning to Understand Commitment 31
6. Conducting the Search 37
7. After the Search 43
8. Counseling as an Art 49
9. Dealing with People 54
10. Sin is the Problem 62
11. You Must Become an Interpreter 68
12. What Interpretation is All About 74
13. Gracious Goodness 83
14. Worthy Workmen in the Word 90
15. Enriched by the Word Within 97
16. Test Yourself, Counselor 102

INTRODUCTION

When the Spirit of God moved Solomon to write, **Whatever your hand finds to do, do it with all your might**,[1] He was addressing a problem as old as flint knives and as new as tomorrow's super computer chip – the problem of mediocrity. The reason set forth in the remainder of the verse is **since there is no activity or planning or wisdom in the unseen world to which you are going.** He is saying that it will be too late when you have died and gone on to the world to come to lay plans, acquire the wisdom necessary, and do the work you should do, in the way you should do it, now. You can't reach back into time from the world to come; *now* is the time to do what must be done.

The one who settles for mediocrity often tells himself, "I can put off doing what I should do till tomorrow. There is plenty of time." But he thinks arrogantly; he does not know the future. He doesn't even know whether there will be a tomorrow for him. He makes excuses for himself: "I'm too tired to do anything today;" "I'm just not in the mood to get to it." But tomorrow never comes.

I knew men who had much to contribute to the Christian world, who were going to write books but who never did so. They are now in Sheol;[2] they will never be able to do what they might

---

1 Ecclesiastes 9:10. The book of Ecclesiastes is not pessimistic. It is pessimistic about life lived for nothing more than this world alone, which is **vanity.** Rightly understood, however, it is one of the most encouraging books in the Bible.
2 Translated "the unseen world" in the above quotation from Ecclesiastes.

have done while yet here in this world. Such persons did not strive for excellence. Rather, they settled for mediocre lives.

Then, of course, there are those who do produce something, but what comes from their hands is never enough, never carefully crafted, never excellent. What you get from them is always average, run of the mill. There is never anything fresh, never anything that even stresses old truths in a new way, never anything ground breaking, never anything that charts a new biblical course.

I am not talking about unbelievers; those to whom I refer are part of the church of Jesus Christ. In view of Christ, Who always did **all things well**, how can those who have trusted in Him for salvation seek to follow any lesser example? True, none of us since the fall is able to attain to His standard of excellence. But under the direction of His Word and in the power of His Spirit we ought to strive to do whatever He has called us to do with all the wisdom and ability we can muster. There is too much mediocrity in the Church.

Nowhere is this problem more evident than in the area of Christian counseling. Some of the difficulties of which I am speaking may, in part, stem from a false worldview which teaches that God reveals truth through unbelievers by means of common grace;[3] I suspect more frequently it is laziness that drives men to adopt or adapt the work of others. They do not wish to engage in the hard tasks of digging out the data, thinking through its relationship to the lives of counselees, and organizing the same into a system of counseling that is based solely upon the truths set forth in the Bible. That takes effort – much more effort than those who pursue an eclectic approach wish to expend. Any miner will tell you that mining is hard work. To mine the Scriptures, and to develop a method and practice of biblical counseling derived therefrom, is no less work. It requires doing something **with all one's might**.

---

3 Revelation is initiated by God and always is inerrant; unbelievers' discoveries, which they themselves initiate, are always subject to error.

This book is designed to encourage and challenge counselors who want to be biblical to settle for nothing less than a ministry of lasting value for the church. It is my hope that it will inspire many to reach for the zenith – to pursue excellence in counseling.

Chapter 1

WHY ALL THE FUSS?

What's it all about? Why should there be so much concern for excellence? What is it that you are attempting to accomplish? Why shouldn't I settle for something less? Everyone can't attain to high ideals, can he? Isn't there a place for those who are willing to settle for less? After all, I'm not interested in notoriety, fame or praise. I'll readily agree to live the quiet life of the "average" person – whatever that may be.

Whoa! Slow down. It's time to get a few things straight. It's true that you should not strive for fame; but if it comes, you ought not despise it. It's true that there is a place for "average living" in some areas of life. You don't have to be an excellent carpenter – if carpentry isn't your life's work. You don't have to be a seamstress – if you only occasionally sew something. But when it comes to what God has called you to do, that is a different matter.

When God calls you to do a task, you must attain to the highest level that you can in pursuing it – for His Name's sake. That is true of counseling as well as any other calling. If God has called you to the ministry of counseling, you are not free to be mediocre. To please Him you must excel. Moreover, as in every area in which others' lives are at stake, you cannot sluff off what you do as "just another thing" among many. You must *give* yourself to the work. What you do has eternal consequences!

Because the glory of God and the welfare of other Christians hangs on it, you must endeavor to become as effective as you can in the task. John Calvin writes of teachers who are like householders "who...have a store laid up for the nourishment of others; and who...make provision for a future and distant period...the teachers of the Church ought to be prepared by long study for giving to the people, as out of a storehouse, a variety of instruction concerning the word of God, as the necessity of the case may require...a varied and manifold distribution, wisely and properly adapted to the capacity of every individual."[4]

He is describing a minister of the Word who is prepared to meet every case individually from the Word of God. In his view, this minister is rarely stumped by the variety of circumstances he encounters, but is ready for them all because he has been diligent in learning all he can beforehand. As a result, he can reach into the storehouse of truth he has compiled to find just the right thing to offer in each instance. Moreover, as Calvin says, he knows how to *adapt* that truth to each *individual* according to *his capacity*. Calvin's description easily fits that of the competent counselor. Obviously, he is not speaking of one who barely gets along in mediocre fashion, but of one who counsels with excellence. That is the counselor you must seek to become. That is what the fuss is all about.

It is important to recognize that God chose to work through human beings. He chose to use people like you and me to minister His Precious Word, to build up His church, and to help one another in time of need. Why? Why? Why? That is a largely unanswerable question. Why, when we are so weak, so ignorant, so sinful? Why, when we are so lazy, so ineffective – so false? Why, when we are so unreliable, so biased, so corrupt? Why you? Why me?

---

4 John Calvin, Commentary, Vol. 16, p. 134.

God could have written truth in the sky, sent angels to proclaim it, or zapped it into our thick skulls! But He didn't. Instead He commissioned people like us to become stewards of the truth. In part, He explains this extraordinary decision: **We have this treasure in clay pots** *so that* **the surpassing greatness of its power may be God's and not ours** (II Corinthians 4:7). God wants others to know that human wisdom administering human ideas does not change lives. Rather, it is His truth, ministered in the power of the Spirit that changes lives. When you look at the minister, you can readily ascertain this fact. He is but a **clay pot**.

But there is another reason for using human beings to counsel others according to God's Word:

> *God chose what the world considers foolish things to put wise men to shame. God chose what the world considers weak things to put strong things to shame.*
>
> (I Corinthians 1: 27, 28)

God is concerned to put the unbiblical counselor to shame. The unbeliever has set up his systems of thought and practice in opposition to that which God has given us. God, therefore, is interested in showing how His Word emerges unscathed from the contest as the true and effective one. But how can He do so, if His Word is garbled and ineffectively presented by those who minister it?

Indeed, in this task of changing men through men, God even established a church that He staffed with elders to rule over His flock who, as Paul said when addressing the church, **labor among you, and manage you, and** *counsel* **you** (I Thessalonians 5:12). Clearly, counseling is the work of the church and *specifically* of those in it who have been appointed and ordained to do so.

The word used in the quotation just given is *noutheteo*. It is the word from which we have derived the name "nouthetic counseling." I hear all sorts of definitions bandied about as to what this word means. Many of these are quite defective, so let me be clear about its meaning. By *nouthetic* counseling we mean the person to person process whereby one Christian CONFRONTS another with Scriptural truth out of CONCERN for him in order to CHANGE him so that he CONFORMS more closely to it. Such nouthetic confrontation is one of the loving tasks assigned to an elder.

While elders are officially given the task of counseling members of the flock, God also expects all the members of every congregation to counsel each other *informally*. This is clear from Romans 15:14 where we read:

> *I, myself, am convinced about you my brothers, that you yourselves are full of goodness, filled with all knowledge, and competent to counsel.*

But notice, even when speaking to ordinary members of the church who are not elders ("**brothers**"), a stress is placed upon **competence**. The word used in Romans 15:14 means "ability" (to counsel effectively). While the nonordained Christian does not counsel with the same authority as that of the elder (cf. Hebrews 13:17), he nevertheless is still called to counsel other Christians.[5] So, the call for excellence in counseling is not exclusively for some small group known as "counselors;" it is for the whole church. If *all* Christians are to counsel well, surely those especially called to the work should excel.

If that is so, Christian, isn't it time to assess your counseling capabilities? Everyone who honestly does so quickly recognizes his deficiencies and his need to grow. In fact, when you frankly assess what you do in counseling, aren't you utterly amazed that anything good ever comes from it? Aren't you again and again impressed with the truth that it is the Spirit using His Word that brings about the changes,

---

5   Cf. also Galatians 6:1ff. On this verse, see my book *Ready to Restore*

and not you yourself? If not, you have pride to repent of before you go any further. Surely Paul was right in characterizing us as **clay pots** in which He has deposited His exceedingly great **treasure!**

Are you of no account then? Can you leave everything to the Holy Spirit to accomplish when you counsel? Absolutely not. Does it matter whether or not you are effective? Yes, it does. God doesn't want you to continue to be ignorant, sloppy and sinful so that He can demonstrate what He can do *in spite of* what you are. Rather, He wants to demonstrate what He can do through you by making something useful of you – in spite of what you have been.

In I Timothy 4:15 Paul exhorts the young minister to become more effective **so that** [his] **progress may be evident to all**. The word translated **progress** has the idea of cutting fresh trails into brand new territory. Somewhat anachronistically, I admit, I picture someone hacking through lush underbrush with a machete. One thing is sure: if your counseling this year is not noticeably different from what it was last year, something is wrong. There ought to be **evident progress** that is noticeable to **all**. Is this true of you? Or is there much work for you to do? To achieve excellence in counseling, there must be continued progress.

Can you do this all by your own effort? Of course not! That is what we have been saying all along. It is God who *uses* His people to minister by making them what they ought to be. When you recognize the enormity of the task and your many deficiencies, don't you cry out with Paul and his companions, **who is sufficient** [*hikanos*] **for these things?** Well, listen to Paul's words in response:

> *...not because we are self-sufficient, thinking that we could accomplish anything by ourselves, but rather because our sufficiency is from God...who has made us sufficient servants of a new covenant.* (II Corinthians 3:5, 6)

So, in spite of – perhaps we ought to say *because of* – our insufficiency there is hope!

Chapter 2

COMMITTED TO CRAFTSMANSHIP

So far we have noted the need for counseling and for competent counselors while underscoring the fact that we are all incompetent and need to grow. How does the growth that leads to noticeable progress take place? How does God achieve this growth in us? Where must one begin? Those are the matters we shall begin to take up in this second chapter.

For starters, you must come to the conclusion that God expects you to commit yourself to craftsmanship. In Proverbs 22:29 He asks, "**Do you see a person skillful in his work? He will stand before kings; he will not stand before obscure persons.**" Are you tired of taking your automobile to be fixed only to have it returned in a condition as bad as it was – or worse? I once owned an Audi Fox. It spent more time in the repairman's garage than in mine! I finally sold it when on its last trip from the repair shop I could take the key out of the ignition, and it would still continue to run until I pushed the light switch button! Incompetence is all around us today because very few persons are committed to craftsmanship. That is why they are not **skillful in their work**.

The ministry of God's Word to people in need is *your* **work**, Christian. The Hebrew word translated **work** means, "work, task, business, ministry." There is a lot of interest in politics today, but what you do in the counseling room is more important than what politicians do in the smoke-filled chambers of the world. Historians here may never record it, but it bears a prominent place in the history books of heaven. You may not slack off on your work. God expects you to use His Word **skillfully**.

The word for **skillful** that appears in Proverbs 22:29 is the third important term that we have encountered so far. In Romans 15:14 (mentioned in the last chapter) the first term, **competent**, is *dunamai,* which means "to be able to accomplish something." The second term in II Corinthians 3 and 4 translated **sufficient**, is *hikanos*, meaning "to have what it takes to get a job done." Here in Proverbs, we find the third term *mahir* which means "skillful, expert, proficient." Notice how the Bible speaks of the need for excellence by means of several words – each of which contributes to the general idea of excellence.

The root of the word *mahir* means "quick" (translated in the Septuagint by the Greek word *oxon*, "sharp").[6] You take your car to a master mechanic (there are a few still around). The motor is going "chuck-a-chuck, chuck." He listens for a second and then tells you to shut it off for a moment. He lifts the hood, fiddles around with something or other, then confidently closes it. He says. "Fire it up again." You do, and instead of "chuck-a-chuck, chuck" you hear "Purrrrrrrrrr!" Ah, for the mechanic who can find and fix the problem quickly and satisfactorily! As Keil and Delitzsch in their Commentary on Proverbs 22:29 say, a *mahir* person is one who has the "technical mastery of something." That means that he knows the *what* and the *how* of the task set before him. To achieve this mastery so as to excel in counseling, one must be committed to craftsmanship.

How can you identify one who (because he has become so committed) has come to excel as a counselor? Among other things, excellence in counseling means to be quick and able in:

---

6 We too call one who is quick and able "sharp." In contrast, we call others "dull tools."

- analyzing a counselee's problem(s);
- giving a biblical description of the problem(s);
- reaching biblical solutions to the problem(s);
- providing biblical implementation for these solutions;
- dealing with counselees as individuals.

All of this is the opposite of "sloppy agape." You must never expect the Spirit to do *for* you what God expects *you* to do.[7] You minister ("serve"); He blesses the Scripture that you minister.

Notice from Proverbs 22:29 that God blesses the outcome of ministry that is skillfully carried out. He says that the *mahir* person **will stand before kings** and will **not stand before obscure persons.** The outcome is expressed both positively and negatively. To **stand before** means either to hold a high office under or come to the attention of a king. Even though there are very few kings around today, and those are far removed from most of us, the principle is clear: the *mahir* man will bear influence in important places.

Have you never been able to make much impact upon your community? Perhaps that is because you have not yet become *mahir*, or not yet *mahir* enough. At any rate, the promise of God is explicit. Putting it negatively, Proverbs says the skillful person **will not stand before obscure persons.**[8] That is to say, neither he nor his work will go unrecognized.

So, if commitment to craftsmanship is where the route to excellence begins, it is important to ask whether you have made such a commitment. We will determine what that commitment involves later: first let us consider a false turn that can sidetrack you.

---

7 God allows for no such expectations, but the Spirit may work in spite of you, if He wills.
8 Lit., "persons in the dark."

Chapter 3

THE THREAT OF ECLECTICISM

Alluring as it may be, eclecticism is a serious threat. It is a decided hindrance to achieving excellence in biblical counseling. The eclectic way offers encouragement from professionals and highly recognized degrees leading to plush positions and money. It requires little original thought and demands virtually nothing in the way of character growth. As a result, it is precisely the place for those who are not willing to make a commitment to biblical craftsmanship.

There has always been a sinful tendency among God's people to abandon God and His Word for something else. The entire Old Testament is replete with incidents of the sort. Speaking for God, Jeremiah puts it this way:

> **My people have committed two evils: they have forsaken Me, the Fountain of living waters, and they have hewn out for themselves cisterns, broken cisterns, that cannot hold water.** (Jeremiah 2:13)

This is a serious problem that has plagued the church of Christ ever since counseling began. The problem with eclecticism is that it is based on the idea that the wisdom of man may be blended with the wisdom of God to produce a third and better thing than either provides alone.

In Acts 17:18 the philosophers in Athens used a derogatory word to describe the apostle Paul. They called him a *spermalogos*.

The Threat of Eclecticism

This term I have translated "an eclectic babbler" in my *Christian Counselor's New Testament*. It describes exactly what the eclectics do. The word pictures a bird going about picking up various sorts of seeds here and there. That, at its core, is eclecticism – it is filling the pot with a little.

Rogers, a dash of Freud, some Maslow, a pinch or two of Adler and a sprinkling of Scripture. Then the whole is mixed together and poured out into a pan to harden. But that simply should not be done. God tells us that in His Word **everything** necessary **for life and godliness** may be found (II Peter 1:3).[9] The eclectic procedure runs counter to Peter's statement. Indeed, to add to the words of the living God is nothing less than unbelief. It is an act of rebellion. Isaiah describes God's people as **rebellious children** when they engage in this sort of thing (Isaiah 30:1). He decries the fact that they **go down to Egypt** to **make counsel** that He says **is not** [His]. He speaks negatively of the alliance they make with Egypt as **weaving a web** that is **not of** [His] **Spirit**. That is, such a thing is not of His doing. Why? How is that rebellion? He goes on to say, that His people **didn't ask for a word from** [His] **mouth** (v. 2). In other words, they trusted in the promises and schemes of the Egyptians rather than in the word of God. As Isaiah also points out, **the Egyptians are men and not God** (Isaiah 31:3). What utter foolishness! Why turn to the words and wisdom of men rather than to the words and wisdom of God? The entire second chapter of I Corinthians denounces the very same thing. And the Psalmist opens the book of Psalms warning against the **counsel of the ungodly**, urging the reader instead to **delight in the law of the Lord**.

The importance of this matter cannot be overstated. The entire church of the Lord Jesus Christ is filled with the ideas of men, largely brought in by so-called "Christian counselors." One does

---

9 See also II Timothy 3:15ff.

not question the salvation of these *spermalogoi*,[10] but he must not approve of their thinking in this matter. Rather than calling themselves "Christian counselors," they more properly might refer to themselves as Christians who are eclectic counselors. But because they (wrongly) use the title "Christian counselors" they deceive many – often including themselves. It is not a matter of their motives, but it is a matter of their commitment to biblical counseling.

It is impossible to grow as a biblical counselor, making **evident progress** toward excellence, when one continually compromises his counseling with a mixture of alien elements. Take, for instance, the idea that one's past must be investigated in detail in order to help solve his problems today (an essentially Freudian concept widely propagated within the church). When one subscribes to this idea, he will spend inordinate amounts of time attempting to do the impossible. No one can trace back all the past experiences that have led to a person's becoming what he is today. It would take as long to do so as it did for one to live through them (or longer). Then at the end (which he could never reach because while following up leads his counselee would be experiencing new events that would need to be tracked down – *ad infinitum*), how would he know that he didn't miss the most crucial experience?

No, going outside of the Scriptures is very harmful to progress in biblical counseling. It has deleterious effects in other areas as well. Consider but one. Delving into the past to find the reasons for present behaviors (attitudes, beliefs, etc.) is a method that seems designed to provide excuses[11] for a counselee. After all, if someone (or something) did it to him in the past, he is probably stuck with it for life. Very little (if any) change can be expected. He is a victim rather than a violator. He is a pawn to be pushed about by people and circumstances. Since this concept runs counter to all that the

---

10   *Spermalogoi* is the plural of *spermalogos*.
11   Doubtless it was so designed by the evil one.

The Threat of Eclecticism

Bible teaches about **human responsibility and change,** it impedes the pursuit of excellence in biblical counseling. Unfortunately, too few of the *spermalogoi* seem to understand this fact.

Now, what I have looked at in terms of one concept eclectically brought into the church may be multiplied many times over. And all of it keeps one from a true commitment to biblical *craftsmanship.* The entire process is deceptive. Most counselors who adopt the eclectic stance have no idea of the damage that they are doing to their counseling ministries and to their counselees. The Spirit of God produced His Word over a long period of time. He, Himself, declared that it makes the counselor **adequate,** and **equips him fully for every good work.** The work in view is the work of changing people by means of the Scriptures (for details, see my book *How to Help People Change,* which is devoted to the exposition and application of II Timothy 3:15-17 in counseling).

Moreover, the eclectic counselor must necessarily hold contradictions. You cannot say that all things necessary for life and godliness are found in biblical **promises** on the one hand, and then on the other hand, search for worldly wisdom that will add necessary dimensions to what you read in the Bible. That is but the beginning of the contradictions that abound in this approach.

In addition to holding confusing contradictions, the *spermalogoi* are themselves personally influenced by the principles and practices of the world as they imbibe and practice them in their counseling. A person cannot spend years in training of any sort and not be influenced by it. And when day by day he works in the atmosphere of those principles and practices, advising others to follow them, his influence is deepened. Whether it is the direct influence of teachers and associates or the continued influence of the pagan system, the truth of I Corinthians 15:33 applies: **"Don't be misled; bad companions corrupt good habits."**

The warning is apropos. The eclectic counselor is **misled**. He may not realize it, but over time he will be led farther and farther away from the pure simplicity of the Scriptures into the world of human wisdom. His whole life will be affected by it. Often this defection takes place over a long period of time. Incrementally, as more and more he lays the Bible aside preferring to study the books of men whose views are in competition with God, his home life, his relationship to the church and other Christians, and (preeminently) his relationship to God are affected adversely. If he doesn't divorce his wife (as far too many have done), he may effectively divorce himself from God and His people. Even when he doesn't go that far, the little worldly beliefs that continually fill his heart and soul harden him to God's word. He may eventually become an adversary of the biblical pastor who attempts to be faithful to Scripture.[12] In some ways, the one who runs off with his secretary is better off – at least he is aware of the radical changes that have occurred.

The incremental changes in one's orientation are described by the Psalmist who speaks of **walking**, **standing** and (at length) **sitting**. Here is a dangerous progression. First, one becomes enamored with ungodly counsel and walks toward it. Next he is fascinated by it and stands there eating it up. In the end, he himself becomes a teacher sitting in the seat, scornfully speaking against that which he once held to.

I am not saying that this course is inevitable; it is my sincere hope that the words of the psalmist may jolt some of those walking along the road toward the wisdom of the ungodly and cause them to turn back. It is also my hope that some of those who have become enamored by such teachings may wake up. I even have an outside hope that some who now scoff may come down from the seat of the scornful. Since the Spirit of God is at work great things are possible!

---

12 He may at length **sit in the seat of the scorner** (Psalm 1:1).

Why, then, do I say that progress toward excellence in biblical counseling is impossible for the eclectic? Because so long as he continues his *spermalogic* course, he is heading in the wrong direction. You cannot go east and west at the same time (without coming apart). You cannot serve two masters. You will come to love one and hate the other. And that is exactly what happens. If one is making **evident progress** in biblical counseling, he is in retreat from eclectic counseling. If he is progressing toward the seat of the scornful, he is leaving biblical counseling behind. Which way are you traveling?

Chapter 4

WHAT DOES A BIBLICAL COUNSELOR DO?

In the last chapter we have seen that (as Jeremiah put it) eclecticism can't hold water. We might even say that it's not all it's cracked up to be. It is both ineffective and, for the Christian, rebellious to **hew out cisterns, broken cisterns that cannot hold water**, when God has provided an abundance of **living water** upon which He bids us draw. What, exactly, do eclectic counselors do? Well, there is no one answer to that question. Some meditate; others medicate. Some hypnotize; others hypothesize. Some correct; others reflect. And some do a little of each. In other words, when you go to an eclectic counselor, unless he tells you up front that he is a disciple of Adler or Maslow or someone else, you can never know what approach he will take. That is the nature of the problem.

There has been a sequence of dominant views running from Freud to the present in which Jung, Rogers, Skinner, Ellis, Bern, Adler, Maslow, and others have for a time held sway. The eclectic counselor who wants to stay up to date has had to retool with each ensuing fad. He has moved from depth psychology through reflective, existential psychology into third force psychology to the mishmash that exists today. Some abandon previous beliefs and practices for the newer ones that come along. More frequently, perhaps, others hold to some of their past views while bunging in some of the newer ones. As a result, today there is such a smorgasbord of offerings that it is hard to describe what system a person accepts.

One Christian who is a popular counselor bases his beliefs fundamentally on Adler. But there is a bit of Ellis, a bit of Freud, and a bit of Maslow mixed in as well. Oh, and there is a bit of misinterpreted and misapplied Scripture too! What would you call him? There is no way to describe what he purports. Another well-known Christian counselor uses different systems for different people as he thinks they apply to each. In his case, though he may use run of the mill Freudianism (with no Bible inserted) with one counselee, it is conceivable that he will mix biblical teaching in with what he does when counseling another person (though, from his writings, I'm sure that he will misapply Scripture as he does). It is a confusing mess out there. You will have people emphasizing the self-talk of Backus, the security and significance of Adler, or the self-esteem and needs teaching of Maslow. There is no consistency anywhere among eclectic counselors in the Christian community. How can a counselor pursue excellence when he is always forced to change his views and start over again with new ones? The idea is preposterous.

But there is one place to turn, where there not only is consistency, but where there also has remained the same root thought and practice throughout all of the changes that have taken place in this past century. That system, precisely because it does not change, allows for a deepening of a counselor's understanding and a growth in his ability. It is a system that, because of its consistency, allows a potential counselee to pretty well know what he will be getting into when he comes for help.

What is that system? It is the system that directs counselees to the Fountain of living waters. It is the system to which counselors who have abandoned the broken cisterns have turned. It is truly biblical, Christian counseling. It is counseling that from start to finish is founded upon Scriptural principles and practices. It is exegetically based. It is theologically competent. It is anchored in eternal truth that does not change. It is counseling that calls upon God through His Spirit to bring about the changes that counselees need to make in order to please Him. Its goal is for His people to become ever more biblical in obedience to God for their blessing. Because counselors of this sort view the Bible as the Book of truth, they cannot mix this truth with the foul sludge of worldly views that is dredged up from what is left behind in those mucky cisterns to which Jeremiah refers.

"OK," you say, "You have made your point. But what does a *biblical* counselor do? To ask it differently, and more pointedly, what does the *Bible* direct a Christian counselor to do?" We will now consider this important question.

It is important to learn just how God Himself describes counseling in the Bible. If you are to become a counselor pleasing to Him, committed to biblical craftsmanship, growing toward excellence, it is imperative to be absolutely sure that you have the correct picture of counseling in mind. Let's consider Isaiah 40:13, 14.

In this place God's infinite knowledge and wisdom is in view. Isaiah is making the point that no one ever teaches or has taught God anything. Obviously, He never needed instruction; He always has known all things. In making his point, Isaiah asked,

> *Who has directed the Spirit of the Lord, or who has, as His counselor, instructed Him? Whom did He consult so as to impart understanding to Him, showing Him the path of justice, teaching Him knowledge, and indicating the way of discernment?* (Berkeley version).

In this passage, incidentally, God sets forth the nature of true counseling. He lists the activities that He expects a counselor to engage in. They are plainly set forth. Notice the operative terms that

What Does a Biblical Counselor Do?

are used: a counselor **directs, instructs, imparts understanding, shows the [right] path, teaches knowledge**, and **indicates the way of discernment**. That is a most instructive list. It is highly descriptive and gives a very clear picture of what biblical counseling ought to involve. There is nowhere a more comprehensive statement about counseling to which one may turn, knowing that it is God's view of what genuine counseling is like.[13] It is, in effect, an inspired description of counseling. So, if one's counseling does not fit the divine description given here, clearly there is something wrong with it.

Let's examine that list for a moment. Notice that all of the words are directive in nature. All Rogerian non-directive notions, therefore, are totally foreign to the biblical concept. Moreover, information and direction flows from the counselor to the counselee. There is no seeking of answers from within the counselee. The counselor is represented as one who already knows what the counselee needs to learn. He is like the scribe mentioned by Calvin (referenced in chapter one on) who has a storehouse of information from which he can instruct according to the needs and capacities of each counselee. That means that the biblical counselor must be one who possesses a solid, working knowledge of biblical truth and knows how to help people to understand and walk in it. As Jesus put it, he is able to **teach to observe**.[14] Unlike God, people *learn* from counselors. If anything, that is presupposed in the Isaiah passage. They acquire knowledge, gain discernment, and come to understand things they did not understand before. They are shown the right paths to follow and directed about how to walk in these paths. Essentially a counselor is a teacher of knowledge, insight, and discernment, who gives advice about how to apply these things and implement them in daily life. We assume then, that these key elements of counseling are those in which one must

---

13 See Isaiah 41:28 in which the counselor also *answers* questions.
14 See my book *Teaching to Observe*

seek to excel. They constitute the craftsmanship to which one must commit himself.

To pursue excellence in biblical counseling means to become *mahir* (proficient) in these tasks and thus to be *hikanos* (sufficient) so as to have the *dunamis* (ability) necessary to carry them out.

It is to **skillful** counseling that God calls you. How skillful are you? What do you need to learn? This book will help you. But it cannot do for you what you must do for yourself.[15] You must be committed to craftsmanship – nothing less!

> BIBLICAL COUNSELING IS HELPING SOMEONE EXPERIENCE GOD'S HEALING TO FREELY LIVE IN LOVE & TRUTH — THROUGH THE SPIRIT. HELPS PEOPLE ID & MOVE OUT OF THE WAY HURTS ~ RESENTMENTS ~ HATERED (OF SELF OR OTHERS OR GOD) → EPH 8:10
> FORGIVENESS   JN 10:10   HEB 4
>
> EXCELLENCE ... YES!

---

15 But remember Philippians 2:13.

Chapter 5

BEGINNING TO UNDERSTAND COMMITMENT

We have been considering the necessity of pursuing excellence through commitment to biblical craftsmanship, the consequences of doing so, and some of the areas in which prayerful effort must be made. Now we want to consider how to go about it.

We shall consider Ezra, as a powerful, concrete example of one who sought and obtained *mahir* status in the eyes of God. Why Ezra? Why not abstract principles? Because not only does the Bible call Ezra *mahir* but because it also sets forth the principles by which he actually attained this level of skill. You have it all bundled up together in Ezra 7:6 where we are told that **Ezra** was **a *mahir* [skillful] scribe in the law of Moses.** Clearly (as we have already seen) if one is to counsel biblically, he too must become skillful ("proficient") in his understanding and use of the Scriptures. Then he will be able to counsel others in meeting individual problems out of a storehouse of information and by means of those skills, as the word *mahir* indicates (and as Isaiah says) a counselor should.

How may we attain to excellence? We are told that **Ezra set his heart** on becoming *mahir* (Ezra 7:10). **Setting the heart on** something scripturally means a fixed determination: it was a heart's desire to which Ezra was committed. He firmly fixed this goal as his calling in life.

From this we see clearly that halfhearted efforts will not prevail. Many have desires, but have little or no commitment. They will not attain to those desires. Vacillation, spreading one's self too thin, or anything that might hinder him from attaining his object must be eliminated. Because too many Christians become caught up in other things, they wander from the path that leads to competence and excellence. They get caught up along side trails or take on too much to achieve anything in any one area. Like someone training for the Olympics, Ezra avoided all of these pitfalls. He knew where he was going, planned how to get there (as we shall see), and stayed the course.

In retirement, I decided to take up the banjo. When I went to my instructor, I made it clear to him that my object was not to become a proficient banjo player. All I was interested in was learning to strum enough chords to be able to accompany myself in humming or singing tunes. I was not at all interested in excellence. I am learning to play for my own amazement! My expressed concern was something far short of excellence. I was in no way committed to craftsmanship. I just wanted to learn a few things about playing the banjo. I simply didn't intend to put out much effort to learn more; banjo playing was a side issue with me. I did not **set my heart** on becoming a *mahir* banjoist. I was happy to be able to play "Happy Birthday" at family gatherings. That kind of relaxed, minimal goal is exactly what hinders so many counselors from becoming proficient in counseling.

By way of contrast, if one wants to **make evident progress** in biblical counseling, he must take a different tack. Like Ezra, he must **set his heart** on becoming proficient. Because counseling is a matter of ministering God's Word, and because the lives of people depend on what happens in counseling sessions, this ministry can never become a side issue like banjo instruction. It must consume the one who is determined to become *mahir*.

We have spoken of pursuing excellence in biblical counseling. The biblical term that runs throughout the New Testament for "pursuing" means "to hunt down until you find." It is a strong word. It conveys the ideas of effort and determination in the hunt. In certain contexts it can even mean "to persecute." To pursue excellence is to be like a hunter who will not give up until he has found and bagged his prey. The person who is determined to become proficient in biblical counseling must not give up either. Through times of discouragement, trial and distraction, he must not allow these things (or any others) to deflect him from his purpose.

On what was it that Ezra set his heart? The goal that he placed before him consisted of three elements. He set his heart (i.e., determined) to

1. study (better, "seek" – dig out the facts of) God's law;

2. do it (i.e., "observe" or obey it: cf. Matthew 28:20);

3. teach it (to God's people).[16]

It is important to understand that these three elements must be a part of every person's determination if he wishes to excel in biblical counseling.

Notice how the three things work together. First, if one has little information, understanding or familiarity with the Bible, it should be obvious that he can neither live according to it, nor teach it to others. Today there are many helps available to aid one in gaining a wide understanding of the Bible that Ezra didn't have. Yet under much more difficult circumstances he persevered. The counselor must have that sort of understanding. In some ways the counselor's breadth of understanding must be larger than that of a

---

16 Biblical counseling is not for unbelievers; we *evangelize* them.

preacher. The preacher (we hope) knows beforehand what he will say when he mounts the pulpit. The counselor, on the other hand, may not know the scope of the counselee's problem until he ferrets it out. His preparation, therefore, must be of a more general sort. There are few surprises for the preacher in the pulpit; in counseling, unexpected elements are often the rule rather than the exception. The range of problems that the Christian counselor encounters is vast. So to become *mahir* in counseling, one must have a broad knowledge of the Scriptures. Therefore, in his quest to become competent to counsel he must **seek out** all sorts of information that a preacher as such (were he not involved in counseling)[17] might postpone studying. The counselor does not have that luxury. He must acquire much data quickly. The honor of God and the welfare of His people are at stake. He may never slacken the desire to know more.

Just what does the Hebrew mean when it speaks of **studying (seeking) the law of God?** It is not the idea of finding that which is lost in the sense of locating the Bible. However, there was such a great famine of knowledge of God's word in Ezra's time that it might as well have been lost. It had been out of sight, it had been left untaught, and the people were ignorant of it. In a sense, then, Ezra truly had to seek (look, search for) it. What it had to say was not in the air. That is true today as well. The Bible is not a lost book in our day, of course; but because of the wrong use of it in counseling circles (and many others as well), it might as well be. Therefore, in a somewhat different sense that has many analogous elements, biblical truth must be searched for. Much as in Jesus' time, the Bible has been covered over by the traditions of men. To get to its truth, therefore, a would-be counselor must truly instigate a *search*.

When I read Ezra 7:10, I picture a person digging for buried treasure. He must work at this until he succeeds. There will be

---

17 Every preacher, however, *is* called to counsel.

false starts, locations that do not yield what he is looking for, and surprises along the way. Effort must be expended over a considerable period of time. Yet, since the treasure is there, in time he will strike pay dirt.

But even though the counselor's goal is broad (he must thoroughly know the Scriptural ins and outs of marriage, divorce and remarriage as well as the biblical method of decision making, how to become a good steward of the finances God has given, etc.), he must do intensive work in every area that he might encounter in counseling. And he must do this quickly. There is no way to attain these things but to devote one's self to the project: to **set one's heart** on what it is necessary to obtain, in order to become a **mahir** counselor.

On the other hand, however, he may never "arrive." The **search** is a lifelong endeavor. These two things he must balance properly. A counselor may never conclude that he is finished learning, as did one would-be biblical counselor who told me that with twenty verses he could handle every problem that he encountered in counseling. He needed no more; he had arrived. One reason why I embarked on the writing of the *Christian Counselor's Commentary* series, which covers the entire New Testament and the book of Proverbs, was to make it abundantly clear that all of God's Word is important in counseling. You may wear thin certain pages of certain Bible books, but you may not leave any of them clean. The worn spots may indicate a prevalence of problems that you encountered, but it may also mean that you are relatively unfamiliar with some portions of the Bible. Be sure that the worn sections of your Bible are soiled and ragged for the former reason, not the latter.

There are tribes where people never travel more than fifty miles from their home and think that when they do they have seen the world. Don't let that happen to you. Psalm 119:96 says, **I have seen an end to all perfection; Your commandment is exceedingly broad.** There may be other claims to perfection, the

Psalmist says, but in the end they all prove to have their limits and imperfections. In contrast, the infinite breath of God's knowledge making up the Bible is so great in its extent that one never reaches its "limits." Indeed, the Source of truth from which it was drawn is limitless. Even though God has not revealed all truth in the Bible (cf. Deuteronomy 29:29), what He has revealed, as a portion of His infinite truth which is related to His infinite knowledge, is beyond our finite limits and total comprehension. One may spend a lifetime searching out all the angles of all he wishes to know and, at the end of the day, conclude that he is but scratching the surface. Yet, in spite of the enormous task, one must search and discover all that he can of God's law. The search is never-ending precisely because there is so much territory to cover. Anyone who thinks that there are no more thrilling surprises to encounter in the study has become closed to truth and needs to open his heart and mind once more to the joys of the search.

In this search, one must know how to mine truth from the Bible. He must acquire a method, the tools and the skills to do so. We shall talk more fully about that in the chapter to follow.

Chapter 6

CONDUCTING THE SEARCH

Ezra's commitment to craftsmanship involved three things, as we have seen. He set his heart to **search for** the law of God, to **obey** it and to **teach** it to God's people. As a result he became *mahir* (proficient, skillful) in his understanding and use of the **law** of the Lord (Ezra 7:6, 10). They are the same three things that you must do if you too would become a skillful biblical counselor. We have been considering the first of these three elements: the search. In this chapter, we come to what is involved in the search. Without a method, the proper skills, and tools and resources, the task is virtually impossible.

That means you must know *how* to mine truth from God's Word. Have you ever taken a course in biblical exegesis (how to interpret Scripture)? How many books do you have on your shelf to help you do Bible study? Ezra didn't have such helps available; he had to fathom these things himself. Indeed, he became the father of biblical study in collating and interpreting the Old Testament books that had been written up until his time. You, on the other hand, are in a much more enviable position; there are many books to which you may refer to learn how to do exegesis. Have you ever made the effort to obtain a catalog of Christian books and to peruse the titles available? Do you have a good concordance, and do you use it regularly? Do you have a multi-volume Bible dictionary? How about good commentaries on the various books of the Bible? And what about a course in Greek (or even Hebrew)? A good place to begin is with a simple guide to these resources, like my book *What to do on Thursday*. This book is designed to introduce you to many of these resources and to set forth a simple method of Bible study and exegesis. It also shows how to apply and implement what you learn to life situations. This kind of text will get you started.

You must search with an open heart and mind. You must come to the well with an empty bucket. If you approach the Scriptures with all sorts of biases, looking for what you want to find, you will doubtless do so. Ask God to remove all bias – except that which is fundamental to proper Bible study – the conviction that the Word of God is inerrant and will provide the truth you and your counselees need to conduct their lives in ways that please God. It is hard to divest one's self of prejudice and bias. Of course, you must never try to remove the bias of the truth you have learned previously from the Bible. But you should be willing and ready to revise former incorrect or incomplete interpretations as you learn more. In other words, you must study the Bible humbly, with a teachable attitude, willing to accept whatever you may find there no matter how it may change your thinking or your lifestyle. The Psalmist wrote: **I have bowed my heart to do your statutes – to the end** (Psalm 119:112). That is precisely what we have been talking about.

Some people ridicule those who approach Scripture with this submissive attitude calling them bibliolators. They act as if we worship the Bible, and scornfully say such things as, "The Bible is his paper Pope!" Well it is far better than a fallible Pope! While we do not worship the Scriptures, we recognize with the Psalmist the words of this Book as the very words of God. Therefore, we respect them and **bow** to what God has to say in them. In bowing to the Bible, we are really bowing to the One Who reveals His will in it.

There is a distinction to be made, but there is a reverence to be maintained. We bow to no other book in that way. To **bow your heart to do God's statutes** so long as one lives (**to the end**) is to show deference to the will of God as set forth in the Bible. If the counselor fails to show deference to the Word of God, how can he expect his counselees to do so? A counselor will communicate to counselees the attitudes with which he approaches and uses the Bible in counseling. If he fails to develop a submissive attitude in his relationship to God's Word, he will unwittingly teach his counselees the same attitude. It is important, then, in your search for biblical truth to learn proper attitudes that are essential not only to learning truth but also to communicating it. What you think and do in the privacy of your own study inevitably will appear in your use of the Bible in the counseling room.

In conducting your biblical search, you must search so as to become enlightened. This is a major reason for the search. You do not search to confirm your own prejudices. You search to learn more of what God has to say. This Book is filled with the **knowledge**, **insight** and **discernment** that Isaiah said a counselor ought to be able to impart to his counselees. It charts the course for one's life and directs him to the **paths of goodness, justice and truth** that he must acquaint counselees with. If he is to become a wise counselor, he must be **filled** with these things, as Paul says in Romans 15:14. How else can he acquire personal traits like this? If he neglects the sole source of wisdom and truth, he will only be able to offer the feeble, twisted wisdom of men. To attempt to do biblical counseling apart from a deep knowledge of the Scriptures is like attempting to build a magnificent castle out of wood, hay and stubble. It cannot be done. Why would you choose to attempt an impossible task that will produce nothing but frustration[18] over

---

18 That frustration is manifest in the fact that of all medical personnel, psychiatrists commit suicide most frequently. Moreover, statistics also show that over half of them have been divorced at least once.

one that is difficult but rewarding? It doesn't make sense. And, as Isaiah put it, it is **rebellion**.

In speaking of the enlightenment that a counselor should seek from the Word of God, the Psalmist also says, **Open my eyes that I may behold wonderful things out of Your law** (Psalm 119:18).[19] In light of this verse, your search of the Bible should turn up things that amaze you. If your attitude is correct and your methods proper, over and over again you will find yourself saying "Wow!"

If your search doesn't continually excite a sense of wonder something is wrong. You'd better find out what, and correct it! This is one important test of whether or not you are on the right track. One serious problem like this occurs whenever a person thinks that he has a full and firm grasp on the Bible. If he ever develops an attitude of superiority and control over the contents, he is treading on thin ice. To the contrary, a searching counselor must be subject to and controlled by the Scriptures – just the reverse attitude to the one who thinks he is superior to them. Other things which may block out the excitement of Bible study include having a know-it-all attitude, conducting the search for wrong motives (e.g., to prove someone wrong rather than to prove God right), using poor methods, having the sort of familiarity that breeds contempt, and refusing to repent of sin in one's life.

Sometimes people ask, "Who counsels the counselor?" Of course, there ought to be other brothers and sisters to whom you can turn in need, but the final answer is found in Psalm 119:24: **Your testimonies are my delight and my counselors**. The idea that doing counseling is unbiblical (as some of late have been

---

19 For more information about the Bible, see my book *Counsel from Psalm 119*. The 119th Psalm is a prayer diary of a person who faced all of life with his Bible. Every verse refers in one way or another to the Scriptures. Studying the Psalm is one way to come to a greater appreciation of the Bible.

endeavoring to show) is absurd. Here the Bible itself is described as doing counseling! True biblical counsel delights. Have you ever heard those who use non-biblical data and methods speak in such language? Why don't they? There is nothing about their methods to delight one's soul. There is everything about biblical truth to do so. Christian counselor, you should thank God every day for the privilege of working with material that not only helps others because it is utterly trustworthy but at the same time is a great blessing to you! The poor counselor who has chosen to go some other way is to be pitied. Pray for him – and for his counselees.

Where can you find the answers to the words of those who oppose biblical counseling? Are there ways in which you can prepare for such attacks upon your stance and your methods (assuming what you are doing is correct)? Certainly. Once more, listen to the Psalmist: **I will have a word for the one who accuses me, since I trust in Your Word** (Psalm 119:42). To **accuse** here means "to vilify"; **word** means "response." The word (response) to the word of accusation is found in *the* Word (of God). How perfectly adequate the Bible is! In it you will find all you need to counsel *and, in addition,* all you need to defend biblical counseling. There is no need to turn to other arguments from outside the Book. Even the very application of its principles and the results in the lives of counselees who follow them is a powerful testimony to the truth of Scripture. Paul was very clear about how he defended truth – it was not by the wisdom of men (philosophical or sophistic reasoning) but by the **demonstration of the Spirit** (I Corinthians 2:4). In other words, the proof is in the pudding. When the Spirit of God is at work through His Word, the evidence will be apparent to any and all who wish to know whether these things be so.

We have noted that eclectic counselors must retool every ten years or so as new counseling systems make their appearance and replace the old. The materials in these counseling books, like medical and technological texts, seem out of date before the ink dries on their pages. That will never be true of the materials that the biblical counselor uses. Nothing else is certain, permanent and lasting. All else is unsettled. But the Psalmist has this to say about the Bible: **Forever, Yahweh, Your Word is settled in heaven** (Psalm 119:89). The biblical standard for life and godliness is **settled**. It may never be altered or replaced. There is no need to do so since, unlike other words, it is *God's* Word.

Many counselees are gullible. They need counsel that will make them wise and buttress them against falsehood. The Bible can even enlighten such persons. Indeed, it has just what is needed: **The unfolding of Your Word gives light, making naive people discerning** (Psalm 119:130). As God enables you to understand, you become able to **unfold** (explain and apply) what you have learned in such a way as to **bring light** into the darkened lives of the naive and gullible. You are searching for rock-solid facts when you conduct your biblical search. When you find them, unlike other counselors, you may honestly say, **the sum total of Your Word is true. And every one of Your righteous judgments endures forever** (Psalm 110:16). From beginning to end, the Bible is true. You will never advise a counselee falsely when you faithfully and accurately teach him what the Bible says. Only the biblical counselor can be sure of the counsel he gives.

What a wonderful prospect, then, is yours — to dig more and more deeply into the mine of divine truth! What more could you desire, or **set your heart to search out?** Like Ezra, do so and at length you too will become *mahir!*

TRUE! YOU CAN'T TAKE A CLIENT FURTHER THAN YOU'VE BEEN YOURSELF

Chapter 7

AFTER THE SEARCH

You can't win a football game by studying the rules and learning the plays in skull practice. That is necessary, but it is also futile if you never get out on the field, run the plays in practice, or scrimmage among yourselves. Then, eventually, you must participate in some games. That is what life is like. Those who think that they can counsel by merely reading books, learning what the Bible says about problems, and so on, but who never practice the biblical principles in their own lives, will never excel. As a matter of fact, any counseling they attempt may not be worth a pin.

Ezra knew that. He did not **set his heart** on becoming an academic who talks a good game but knows little or nothing about participating in it. Instead, he determined to **search out the law** of God *and then* to **do it.** One of the problems seminaries have experienced is what is called "field training." Recognizing that students need more than the academic side of their training, some programs call for sending students into the "field" to work alongside pastors in churches. The theory is that the teacher in the seminary presents the academics, the pastor in the church provides the experience. There is, however, one great fault in this process. The students inevitably gravitate to one or the other instructor. They find it impossible to serve two masters. Indeed, they come to love the one and hate the other! Some say, "Ah, the professor at

43

the school is the one who really has it. This man out in the field is only a second-rate hack." Or, on the other hand, there are those who conclude, "No, the professor hasn't really got a clue about ministry. It is the pastor who is with it." The problem is that you have two different persons representing two different sides of one task. What is needed, and is hardly ever found, is the *same* man teaching in the classroom and then taking his students out into the field and showing them how to apply it. Theory and practice must be integrated by the same person. A well-known author and professor once told me, "I like to write about Christian counseling, I don't like to counsel; consequently I don't do counseling." In contrast, at Westminster seminary, we integrated the instruction in counseling for our students. I taught in class, then took students along into actual counseling cases where they could watch me counsel, summarize the case, and then ask me questions about what they had seen and heard. Ezra was studying not merely to fill his head with facts. He was committed to putting into practice what he had learned. He learned for living.

Always, in the Bible, the purpose of truth is for life.[20] Corresponding to Ezra's three purposes: to **search**, to **do** and to **teach**, we might more generally say that *truth* should lead to *life* which, in turn should lead to *ministry*. It is the second of these three elements that are necessary for excellence with which we are concerned at this point: **doing**, or turning truth into life. This is the meaning of the very interesting biblical phrases **walking in the truth** (II John 4) **and doing the truth** (I John 1:6). In Matthew 28:20 the Lord Jesus speaks of **teaching to *observe*** (i.e., to obey, practice).

It is important, then, to understand that everything a counselor learns ought to positively affect his own life. Ezra was careful not to become a hypocrite who learned one thing and lived another. Of course, none of us is able to perfectly accord life with

---

20 See Titus 1:1 where Paul affirms that **truth is in the interest of godliness**.

learning (cf. Colossians 2:6; Philippians 3:16). Every student of the Bible *knows* more than he *does*. But the counselor ought to be committed to doing all that he has learned that God wants him to do from his searching out of truth.

In the academic arena, in which many of us were raised, the goal is to pass the course, to learn the information needed for the next test, or something of the sort. Seldom does a course require the student to become proficient in performing what he had learned he ought to do. Sometimes the idea is truth for truth's sake. However, according to the Scriptures, knowledge is never learned to make one educated. To speak of a "learned" person is to put the emphasis in the wrong place. Learning ought to be for living. If one must learn French and German simply to be allowed to jump through the Ph.D. hoop (as many of us did), the experience is not only grueling, but also practically worthless (since we were never going to use this information we crammed into our heads). Learning ought to be for doing – first in our own lives.

The Bible always assumes that the purpose of learning is to attain **wisdom**. Unfortunately, today we hear virtually nothing about "wisdom." You may read the newspaper from cover to cover for over a year and never encounter the word. You may listen to TV newscasts from now to eternity with identical results. But what is wisdom? A careful study of the Book of Proverbs (and the rest of the "wisdom" literature) makes it perfectly plain that wisdom is the prudent use of God's truth in practical situations. Wisdom, certainly, is what God expects in a would-be counselor. If the counselor cannot apply what he has learned to actual situations in his own life, how will he be able to advise others to do so?

In the Bible, truth comes applied (cf. Philippians 2 where the difficult theological doctrine of the *kenosis*[21] is discovered in

---

21 For details on this see *The Christian Counselor's Commentary* on Philippians

a very practical context having to do with putting others first). Many do not like the form in which the Bible was given to us. They would have preferred an encyclopedia, alphabetically and topically arranged. But God did not choose to provide any such thing. We should learn from the way in which God gave us truth. God presents truth *applied.*

If you study the Bible for personal profit rather than merely to obtain answers to use in counseling, you will be doing three things at once: (1) you will be getting those answers (2) in a practical form that will enable you to better apply them to counseling cases while (3) you will be growing spiritually as a Christian. The way in which you present truth in counseling sessions will be practical. You will know many of the difficulties, wrong turns, potholes, and roadblocks that counselees may encounter in attempting to achieve biblical goals. You will be able to warn about and even make suggestions about how to avoid these problems. The person who has already walked the road can better tell someone else where to go and how best to get there. Never forget II Corinthians 1:3, 4.

You too must learn to do God's will unhesitatingly, fearlessly and enthusiastically, the way Abraham, Paul and Peter did. Otherwise you will find it difficult to ask counselees to do so without hypocritical guilt. And, if you are merely asking (not yourself doing) more often than not, counselees will detect artificiality in what you are saying. This will come to the forefront especially when they ask for help, ask how to pull something off, or the like. If you have not experienced something of the problems they are encountering yourself and overcome them, you will betray your inadequacy.

Listen once more to the Psalmist – a man who you immediately understand *lived* the truths he wrote about: **I thought about my ways and turned my feet to Your testimonies** (Psalm 119:59). The 119th Psalm is so helpful precisely because you realize that the Psalmist is writing about the very things you are experiencing yourself in a way that enables you to apply them to your own situation. As the Psalmist indicates, thinking about Scripture (in the search) should move one's **feet** to follow those **testimonies**. The thoughts of the heart should trickle down into the feet. Once more, listen to what he says: **I will meditate on Your commandments, and I will regard Your ways** (Psalm 119:15). Meditation in the Bible (unlike some modern non-Christian forms of meditation) leads to formulating and carrying out action mandated by the Scriptures. The purpose of meditation is not to obtain some warm feeling, but to determine just how truth should lead to action. One learns truth, meditates on what he has learned in the light of his own circumstances, and then formulates a plan "to put feet on" the truths he has learned.

Speaking of enthusiastic conformity to God's Word, listen to the Psalmist: **I will *run* the way of Your commandments when You will enlarge my heart** (Psalm 119:32). Once his understanding (**heart**) is **enlarged** (expanded by new truth and its implications for his life), he wastes no time putting it into practice. He hurries (indeed, **runs**) to conform his ways to God's will. Elsewhere he puts it this way: **I hurried, and didn't delay, to keep Your commandments** (Psalm 119:60). It is important for every counselor to thoroughly familiarize himself with Psalm 119 if he would be of the greatest assistance to counselees. That is why I have referred so often to this Psalm (for fuller understanding of each verse, see my book *Counsel from Psalm 119*). What does the Psalmist do when others scoff? Does he let up?

Quit? Does he hide his commitment to the Word? Does he follow some other way? Not on your life. He continues to follow God's Word enthusiastically and *fearlessly*: **The proud have completely scorned me; I have not deviated from Your law** (Psalm 119:51). And he applies the Scriptures in time of need: **It is good that I was afflicted that I might learn Your statutes** (Psalm 119:71). Affliction did not move him to abandon God's truth; it drove him deeper into it. As a result, in counseling others, he would find that (in the words of the apostle Paul) he could **help others in all their afflictions** with the **same help with which God helped him** (II Corinthians 1:4).

Clearly all the vital saints in the Bible used God's truth in their lives. This is in stark contrast to the kind of non-applicatory "preaching" abroad which is totally unbiblical. Indeed, this biblical-theological preaching is more like reading an essay than preaching to people about the lives they live before God and their neighbors. Such preachers simply set forth truth and leave the rest to God. A counselor sitting under such preaching (or trained to preach in that style) will be adversely affected. He must reject it if he ever expects to excel in counseling (or, for that matter, in preaching!). When one becomes applicatory in his own life he will begin to become helpful to others. This leads to the third objective that was a part of Ezra's commitment to craftsmanship: teaching others. Without it no counselor will ever become *mahir*.

Chapter 8

COUNSELING AS AN ART

When we talk about improvement in counseling, we must take into consideration the fact that, like painting, counseling is an art. You will fail to appreciate the many nuances of good counseling until you understand this fact. What I mean by "art" is the skill and ability to bring about the intellectually-desired ends to which one aspires.

Accordingly, it is not sufficient to just have the correct goals in mind or simply learn about the processes that are involved in counseling. That is the academic or intellectual approach to counseling. Perhaps the problem is best exemplified in what that well-known teacher of counseling said: "I don't like to do counseling; I like to write about it." No one, it seems to me, can write very convincingly about counseling unless he has been involved in the practice of counseling as well. That is why his books are not only eclectic, but also have about them a wooden artificiality that offers little help to the people out in the trenches. To learn to counsel or, for that matter, to train counselors requires more than "book learning." It is true that a football team engages in "skull practice" before hitting the field. They must know the plays that their coach outlines on the whiteboard. But if they never run through those plays, never engage in scrimmages, never practice over and over throwing the ball or blocking, you can be certain they will lose the game. Something similar to this is true of counseling as well. The would-be counselor must be more than an "armchair" counselor who can talk a good game, but hardly knows what to do in the counseling room.

To return to the image of painting, let's see what is involved in learning an art. A person wants to know how to paint, so he reads up on painting. He may take courses in painting. He learns what perspective means, how to use contrast of color, how to use light and dark, and so on. He acquires a sufficient amount of "head knowledge" of the art of painting. Much like the professor who doesn't like to counsel, he can *talk* painting with you. But his talk is purely academic; it comes from books and the ideas of others. He has nothing to offer from his own experience since it is virtually nil.[22]

In addition to reading and talking about painting, the student must also be able to study significant paintings – preferably under the guidance of an expert painter who will spend time discussing the various elements that constitute each. In this discussion he will also be able to ask questions and receive answers. He may also be able to relate the reading that he has done to the works of art that he studies. He will discover, among other things, that each artist has his own particular ways of painting, some conforming to the theory that he has learned and some not. He will discover also that theory or practice may be suspended for various purposes that the books could not take into consideration since they could not cover every possible painting situation.

Then, having spent considerable time reading, discussing and observing paintings under tutelage, he will advance to watching a painter at work. He will observe how he mixes his colors, how he

---

22 True, there are times when one who is not so fully involved may contribute something from a more "objective" stance, but it will almost always be of a theoretical or technical sort; there will be little help for the practitioner.

holds his brush, how he applies the paint to the canvas, and so on. He will ask more questions about technique and theory as these factors come together in the act of painting. A good teacher will point out what he is doing and why he is doing it, and show him the effects of his work. He will also ask questions of his trainee to see how well he is learning. The responses he receives may lead him to go back over points to emphasize matters not well understood, and this procedure may lead to new discussions of matters that the teacher thought he could take for granted, but found that he couldn't. Questions also may open up issues that might otherwise have been passed by.

Then, after the student has spent adequate time observing, he must take up the brush himself. This also should be under the instruction of a teacher. Otherwise he may develop poor practices from the outset. At times it may be important for the teacher to stop his student with brush in mid air, for instance, saying such things as "Wait! You'll get that all wrong unless you learn to apply the paint differently. Here, let me show you what I mean." That kind of apprenticeship (discipling) is also essential to improvement. Then, when the instructor has successfully inculcated good habits and skills, he may back off for a while, letting his student spend time painting on his own. From time to time he will check out his student's work – commending him on his progress, making corrections and suggestions, and encouraging continued (or greater) diligence.

Finally, the instructor must leave the scene altogether. The former student then must become a teacher himself. He will learn from this teaching (from the necessity to formulate his views and practices in order to teach) further improving his own painting skills and understanding of painting. While helping others to get started, he himself will grow.

All of the elements above should be applied to counseling. If one wishes to become a God-honoring counselor, he must also take similar steps. First, he must study the theory of counseling. I have written extensively to enable one to do this with ease. Then he must observe counseling (as one studies paintings). And unless a counselor is willing to have someone sit in on counseling as a part of the counseling team, this will be hard to bring about. But there are pastors who would be happy to teach their elders how to counsel and there is training available online through the Institute for Nouthetic Studies.[23]

The next stage of counseling after adequate observation is practice in counseling under tutelage. I always made my trainees part of the counseling team – bringing them into the counseling room itself (not hiding them behind a one-way window). Then, as counseling progressed and as a trainee seemed to be catching on, I would find natural opportunities for him to take over counseling briefly.[24] Later on, I might even put a trainee in the counselor's seat from the beginning of a session as I sat by on the sidelines ready to help if necessary. Next he would be given counseling cases, over which I would exercise supervision, discussing them in detail afterwards. Finally, the trainee would be turned loose to train others (always with the understanding that I would be available for help if he became stymied).

This kind of process is necessary for adequate counseling training. The ideal, it seems to me, is to be able to sit in with a local pastor who is willing and able to train during a number of actual counseling cases. Elders, especially, could be trained in this format and would be useful to the congregation as a supplement to the work of the pastor (shepherd-teacher). Something like Jethro's suggestion to Moses seems in order in most churches.[25]

---

23 www.nouthetic.org
24 For instance, if it were necessary for me to leave the room temporarily to write a letter.
25 Exodus 18:13-26.

This last step in the training process is so essential since counseling is an *art* in which – as in all art – the various elements of the practice come together in one person who is actually doing them. On paper they may be spelled out in sequence. In real life, they may all merge in one person, working with God's Word, who is doing all or most of the elements at the same time, as the Spirit also is at work using the Word. This cannot be represented accurately in books – or even in discussions. It must be seen and heard in the counseling room.

Of course, the pastor who trains must be a competent counselor himself. If he is not, he must find a way to develop his knowledge and skills so that he may counsel well and be able to teach those around him. It is the pastor's task to train his leadership and to some extent all of the members of his flock in counseling since good counsel is required of every Christian (cf. Galatians 6:1; Colossians 3:16; Romans 15:14).

Chapter 9

DEALING WITH PEOPLE

For all too long much has been said, without response, about how nouthetic counselors deal with people. "They beat them over the heads with their Bibles" or something akin to this slanderous accusation is frequently heard. That sort of gossip, spread about by persons who have never taken the trouble to learn the truth, certainly has no basis in fact. It is time for the truth to be told. My purpose, however, is not to vindicate biblical counseling or biblical counselors. Rather, it is to set forth the true goals of nouthetic counseling for those who are committed to craftsmanship in counseling. How is it that they should treat counselees? There are few more important questions for the growing or would-be counselor to consider.

Put simply, biblical counselors must endeavor to treat people *precisely as Jesus and the apostles did*. That is the simple but profound standard by which their every relationship in counseling must be governed.[26] Nouthetic counselors have no additional standards (as other counselors do) for dealing with counselees.

---

26 Of course, this standard is no WWJD (What Would Jesus Do?) vagary in which the individual decides on his own what Jesus might have done. Rather, at every turn, decisions are made by exegetical study of the Scriptures.

Dealing with People 55

For example, consider the effects of three of the systems whose ideas are tossed in with Christianity by eclectic counselors. The Freudians will not take counselees seriously about what they say. They interpret counselees' views as rationalizations rather than as facts. On the contrary, the biblical counselor will always take the counselee at his word (following I Corinthians 13:7)[27] unless evidence forces him to reject it. Rogerian counselors will do everything within their power to keep counselees from turning to any outside authority such as the Bible or the church. They abhor and denounce authorities. They want to make people autonomous, looking within themselves for the answers to life. This assault upon the very nature of man as a creature dependent on his Creator does him a great injustice. Strict adherence to this Rogerian standard would prohibit people from hearing the life-giving message of the gospel. Skinner treated man as an animal, and taught his disciples that they must learn to control man by rewards and aversive control (punishment). This view explicitly rejects the image of God in man. It avoids human responsibility and encourages the development of a herd mentality in the counselor. The treatment that results is the same as that which you would not show toward a dog!

It is interesting that those who adopt eclectic views scarcely ever question the ways in which they have been taught to deal with counselees. Yet, you can readily see that what they have been encouraged to do is highly questionable when you give the slightest thought to it. It seems that opprobrium is cast only upon nouthetic counselors – and then for supposed practices that have no basis in fact!

I said that the nouthetic counselor's goal is to treat counselees as the Savior and His apostles would. Of course, that is a big order and one that few of us live up to. We are all sinners who fail but who, in accordance with the teachings of the Bible, willingly admit to failure and seek forgiveness whenever and wherever it is necessary. There is no claim to perfection on the part of those who teach the

---

27 "Love believes all things, hopes all things."

biblical doctrine of the fall. And, quite contrary to what is often said about them, because of this nouthetic counselors acknowledge and understand the problem of human frailty and, with their Lord, show sympathy for counselees as they too undergo temptation (cf. Hebrews 2:18).

So let's say it again: nouthetic counselors are *concerned* about treating people properly. If they are truly nouthetic, they understand that a prominent element in the word *nouthesia* is its familial nuance. This is manifested clearly in the use of the verb in I Corinthians 4:14 where Paul writes, **"I am not writing these things to shame you, but to counsel[28] you as my *dear children*."** Because they counsel only believers [why move unbelievers from one lifestyle displeasing to God to another equally so? (Cf. Romans 8:8)], they confront every counselee as a brother or sister in Christ.[29] Therefore, they must relate to them even more warmly than if they were blood related. As Paul considered the Corinthians family in Christ ("my dear children") despite all their sins and confusion, so too does the Christian counselor. That means that all of the qualities of love, patience, endurance, friendship, hope, and so forth that are enjoined upon Christians in their relations to one another, are also required of counselors when dealing with their counselees. Nouthetic counselors do not forget their spiritual kinship to their counselees when counseling them. There is no cold professionalism in the relationship. With Paul, they **rejoice with those who rejoice and weep with those who weep.** Unlike many other counselors, they become involved in their counselees' lives. It is difficult to truly pray for another – which nouthetic counselors do – and not become involved.

In short, nouthetic counselors seek to love their counselees. I Corinthians 13:4-8[a] sets the standard of love. Love, Paul says, **is**

---

28 The verb here is *noutheteo*.

29 They make no heart judgments; that is God's business. But unless disciplined out of a true church of Christ or having apostatized from it, a counselee is considered a believer if he is a member of it.

patient. That is truly a necessary factor in all successful counseling. Counselees will be slow learners, will regress, will fail, will become stubborn. Counselors must have patience and not lose their cool with them. At times this is very difficult. But the goal is to have perseverance – a decidedly Christian trait. How is it that a nouthetic counselor can show such loving patience when things are not going well?

There are certain presuppositions that underlie his approach. First, as I have noted, he considers the counselee as a spiritual brother. He has loving, brotherly concern for him. Moreover, he knows that the church which he is a member of is suffering to the extent that this member is debilitated by problems. He is concerned to strengthen the church through successful counseling. Most of all, however, he knows that in the life of this counselee the Lord is to be glorified. He is concerned to send him back to his several relationships with a strong testimony to God's grace.

The counselor also is able to persevere in times of discouragement because he believes that if this member of Christ's church is truly regenerate, he possesses all the resources to overcome his problems and to honor God. Within him dwells the Spirit of Christ. That means that he has all the resources that are necessary to interpret the Bible as well as to obey God's commands in it. He knows that the Spirit sanctifies by the Word (John 17:17), which is truth. So he believes that there is every possibility (though perhaps at the moment not readily apparent) for this brother or sister to make the changes necessary. So, in his every relationship with the counselee, the nouthetic counselor seeks to exhibit patience. This patience, however, must not be interpreted as indulgence. There is no place in the Bible where indulgence in sin is commended. Nor should the biblical counselor do anything that encourages such indulgence. He must always be complimenting (where he can honestly do so), encouraging, and instructing (cf. I Thessalonians 5:11, 14). But he must also admonish.

Love is also **kind**. That is what Paul writes. So, in order to show love toward a counselee, the nouthetic counselor seeks to maintain a kind attitude that leads to kind words and actions. This means that he must never be harsh, cruel, or inconsiderate of the counselee. It means that he is to go overboard in attempting to help him solve his problems. It pictures a person who, while telling the truth in all its naked reality, speaks in a kind way – even when he must be firm (cf. Ephesians 4:15). It pictures a relationship with a counselee that is illustrated in I Thessalonians 2:4-12 (carefully read this section if you want to know how to treat counselees).

Once more, Paul says that love **isn't jealous**. There are times when counselors are tempted to become jealous of counselees or other counselors. Either their attainments, their wealth or their fame may tempt a counselor. But there is no place in the work of counseling for any such thing. The true counselor sees that God blesses others as He sees fit and rejoices in it in love. At times, it is easier to weep with those who weep than to rejoice with those who rejoice – especially when the prosperity of a brother or sister is greater than one's own. But, in his attitudes toward others – whether they be counselees or other counselors – he should always show loving joy in their good fortune. Love, Paul says, **doesn't boast, and isn't proud**. A superior attitude toward others has no place in counseling. In love, the counselor shows humility toward his counselees. He is always aware of the fact that his every attainment is purely by the grace of God. In himself, he is utterly unable to achieve anything pleasing to God. He avoids boasting and pride as he seeks to help; his attitude is properly exhibited in Galatians 6:1 where Paul speaks of **a spirit of meekness**. His attitude is that he is no better than his counselee. He acknowledges that, apart from the grace of God, six weeks from now it is possible he too may need counsel. He follows the advice found in I Corinthians 10:12.

Love **doesn't act in an ugly way**. There are counselees who do, but that doesn't mean that the counselor retaliates in kind (he keeps Proverbs 15:1 and Romans 12 in mind). Nor does he become ugly when counselees fail to do what they ought to. He pleads, he urges, he encourages, he admonishes – but never in a hateful or arrogant manner. He really wants to see the counselee succeed. He understands that ugly behavior or words will not accomplish the work of God and will only demonstrate to his counselee attitudes that he wishes for him never to emulate. Instead, he is lovingly firm in those situations where he might be tempted to be ugly.

Love **isn't self-seeking**. The nouthetic counselor always counsels first for the honor of God, second for the welfare of the church, and third for the benefit of the counselee. This he keeps in mind at all times, and it is a factor in all that he says and does. He isn't interested in obtaining money from counselees. As a pastor, he already is paid to minister. He isn't interested in gaining fame or notoriety. He does not publicize himself. He is wary of titles that read: SO-AND-SO'S MINISTRY. He never pushes himself forward, but instead tries to downplay all such efforts on the part of others.

Love **doesn't keep records of wrongs**. This of course means that he has no part in accumulating lists of the ways in which counselees (or others) wrong him. Rather, in accord with the biblical picture, he **covers a multitude of sins** with love (I Peter 4:8). In those cases where sin cannot merely be passed over but becomes a barrier to fellowship, he is willing to follow the injunctions of Matthew 18:15ff. He will not allow an unreconciled condition to persist. Love demands that it be settled (and it doesn't matter who the problem is with: cf. Romans 12:18). In this way he attempts to become an example to counselees.

Love, Paul explains, **isn't happy about injustice but happily stands on the side of truth.** Misrepresentations, dirty tricks, lies, and the like are anathema to the biblical counselor. He is deeply concerned whenever he encounters them in his counselees or in others who have dealings with them. He will always stand on the right side in such matters even when it is difficult to do so. He is never neutral about righteousness. He takes sides – out of love. Truth, justice, and the like attract him. The opposites repel him.

Love **covers all things**. There is no desire to publicize the misdeeds of others. Rather in love they must be covered (but not avoided). They are covered by confession, repentance, forgiveness and reconciliation. All these things are part and parcel of the nouthetic counselor's approach. He understands the biblical teaching about these matters, and advocates and practices according to biblical procedures that grow out of them. The covering is done in a biblical manner – not in a way that ignores or accepts sinful behavior (cf. also James 5:20).

I have mentioned already that love gives the benefit of the doubt to the counselee: it **believes all things, hopes all things.** That is to say, unless there is clear, unmistakable evidence to the contrary, a counselor accepts the statements of the counselee as true. That does not make the counselor a dupe. He is not deceived (if at all) for very long. Homework, based on the data received from counselees, will soon make it clear if there was untruth in the data he received. A lying counselee will not be able to carry it out as designed. When the failure is examined, the falsehood will come to light. But the counselor's fundamental attitude should be belief, the expectation that the words of the counselee are accurate so far as he is able to describe a situation. That attitude on the part of the counselor will encourage truth telling on the part of most counselees.

Paul also declares that love **endures all things**. There is much to endure in counseling: ingratitude on the part of counselees, attacks leveled at you from counselees or others, slander and misrepresentation by those who do not adopt a biblical approach to counseling. But the counselor who honors God doesn't give up. He is grateful to God for His Word and sees the possibilities for strengthening the church and those who need help. He wants to glorify God by doing so. So he endures.

Finally, Paul observes that love **never fails**. When manifested in the ways mentioned above, it not only continues but also always succeeds. *God's* purposes are achieved (cf. Isaiah 55:10, 11). The counselor may fail to help the counselee as he had hoped, but it will not be because of his wrong treatment of him. So far as it depends on him, he will succeed in the relationship that he establishes (Romans 12:18). That means that if the counselee (who may not have been altogether serious about wishing to change) some day does become serious, he is likely to return to the one who lovingly attempted to help him. He will have every reason to do so.

There is much more to say about how to relate to counselees. Usually, misrepresentations come from the fact that nouthetic counselors take the Bible seriously. That may mean that in a given counseling case the counselor will settle for nothing less than what the Bible requires of his counselee. Sometimes stubborn counselees, who dig in their heels against the Scriptures, go away unhappy because they could not make the counselor bend to their wishes. That is the source of some of the gossip about biblical counseling. Other misrepresentations of biblical counseling come from other counselors whose sacred cows have been shown to be unbiblical. Nouthetic counselors (while having sympathy for those who are deluded into following error) have no time for the systems of unbelievers that some bring into the church. These systems are opposed to God and His truth as surely as the beliefs and practices of the Amalekites were. And when biblical counselors say so, that antagonizes those who are deeply invested in them. I challenge you to compare any other system of counseling with the biblical one by applying the principles of love found in I Corinthians 13 to it! I assure you, it will not fare well.

So, to put it all in a nutshell: nouthetic counselors seek to relate to their counselees in love: the love which is taught and demonstrated in the Scriptures.[30]

---

30 Not some sort of ersatz love stemming from another source.

Chapter 10

SIN IS THE PROBLEM

"Aha! There it is – all you people ever look for is sin." I can hear it now. Those who are prejudiced against nouthetic counseling level their gravest charge in saying that we blame every problem a counselee has on sin in his life. Whoa! We never said that. As far back as 1970, when *Competent To Counsel* was first published, I made it absolutely clear that this is not so. In that book I noted the cases of Job and the man born blind (John 9), where in each instance it was clearly articulated that the person involved was not to blame for his condition. His sin was not in question.

"Well, then, what are you saying in the title of this chapter? Either sin is or isn't the problem that counselees have. Explain yourself, please." Sin *is* the problem. There is no counseling difficulty that you will ever face that is not rooted in sin. Bill Goode, former director of the National Association of Nouthetic Counselors, used to say, "Every counseling problem is a theological problem." He was right. But even more specifically, every counseling problem is also a sin problem. There would be no problems, no counselors to deal with them, and no controversy about how to do so if it hadn't been for Adam's sin. Every counseling problem stems from the first sin – the sin in the garden of Eden. That is what I mean by saying that sin is the problem.

All of the problems that we face (physical or spiritual) are the result of Adam's sin – not only those problems that we bring upon ourselves because we were corrupted by the sin of Adam, but also those problems that are occasioned by the sin of others and by God's curse through which the earth was set against us. All of the difficulties, troubles, or problems[31] that we encounter are the result of sin. Hence, the title of the chapter: *Sin is the Problem*.

Note well, I have not said that some specific sin of a counselee is the problem that you will always have to deal with in counseling. It is true that he, as a sinner, will always present certain problems of misunderstanding, false thinking, sinful habits, and so on, that may exacerbate the problem, just as you will discover that sin in your life will make counseling more difficult. But when we are talking about the central problems with which you must deal, we are making it plain that it may not be a matter of the counselee's sin at all. The fundamental problem may be the sin of others against him (his wife's adultery, for instance) and how he should handle it according to God's Word. Secondary problems may arise, as I have said, stemming from the fact that every counselee (and counselor) is a sinner. And, at times, a secondary problem may take center stage for at least a time while you attempt to enlighten or encourage the counselee. But the problem may not be a matter of his own making. That is the point I wish to make. Every biblical counselor must have this clear perception of the counseling situation ever before him as he counsels.

Now, I want to make a second point. Understanding that sin is involved one way or another in all counseling, as I have observed, is a very important advance over all other counseling systems. Most other counselors know nothing of sin. And because this dimension of man's condition is missing from their systems, they fail to understand the true dynamics of counseling problems

---

31 Or whatever term that you wish to use; I am using them synonymously here.

and, therefore, how to deal with them. To grow in the work of biblical counseling you must have a full acquaintance with the biblical data concerning sin and its effects. It is my suggestion that you take time to study the subject in the Scriptures so that you will be able to deal with sin in whatever form and with whatever effects you may encounter in a given counseling case. The concept of sin is a large concept – contrary to what most think who dismiss it in counseling. And it is precisely because they do not take it into consideration that their systems are seriously flawed.

Let's consider that for a moment. One such system says, "Counseling problems have an organic base." In certain cases, that may be true (far less than is claimed). But why do organic problems exist? Because of the curse of God on humanity. There would be no club feet to contend with, no disease to suffer from, no hormonal difficulties to deal with, if sin had not occurred. Because some tend to use sin's effects to justify wrong behavior, they often misinterpret what is happening as being organic in nature. They blame sinful behavior on the organic problem, when that may be the egg, not the chicken. And at times people neglect their duties and shirk responsibilities when they think that they can use an organic difficulty as an excuse for doing so. The main point is that sin is extensive enough to encompass the subcategory of organic difficulties.

Other false counseling systems make the environment the source of all our difficulties. That there is an environment in which we live that is hostile to the ways of God is also a given.[32] It is plain that this environment makes living as a Christian difficult. But we may never blame the environment for our failures or sinful behavior. God's Word has been given in order to enable us to sail between the sandbars and reefs without shipwreck. When we do not, that is not the fault of the environment but of the person who navigates by some other standard than the Scriptures. Again, the

---

32 For more on this see my book *Christian Living in the World*.

concept of sin fully encompasses all environmental problems. There would be no such world if there had been no sin. The present world is one with which God is displeased. He will someday eliminate all that offends and refashion a new world out of the melted down elements (cf. II Peter 3:1-12). Indeed, Adam and Eve were placed in a perfect environment and would have had no problem if they had guarded the garden environment against intruders as God had commanded (cf. Genesis 2:15)[33]. But they did not. Hence, sin is at the root of all environmental difficulties.

I do not think that it is necessary to consider all other counseling systems separately. I think that you get the point from the two that I have just mentioned. No matter what any system sees as the base of a counselee's difficulty, you should realize that it will always ultimately go back to sin. The fundamental problem is not some *effect* of sin (as the advocates of these systems think), but sin itself. Until the practitioners of a system take this fact into consideration, they will fail to ascertain a counselee's true problem. All other systems, focusing on some effect of sin (abuse, wrong thinking, or whatever) merely concern themselves with some manifestation of sin in the world and in the counselee. They fail to penetrate deeply enough to uncover the real problem. They see a part of the whole *as* the whole. They wear blinders; they have tunnel vision. Biblical counseling opens up one's understanding so that he may view the entire field, seeing the big picture. He alone, therefore, is able to apply the correct remedy to the problem.

If every problem is theological and involves hamartiology (the doctrine of sin), then the remedies for counseling problems cannot be only medical, only a matter of changing the environment, or anything that fails to involve God and the redemption and sanctification that is found in Jesus Christ. Biblical counseling, focusing on the underlying problem, forces one to focus also on

---

[33] The word "keep" should be translated "guard" as it is in Genesis 3:24.

the underlying solution. That is why when we say that sin is the problem, we also say that Christ is the solution. We are not problem oriented, but solution oriented. How can we be otherwise when we not only understand the bad news of sin but also proclaim the good news of salvation? Counselors must always reach beyond a sin's effect to its cause.

What does this look like? Take a simple example (by doing so, we can make the principle stand out more clearly). Someone has been sinned *against* – he has been lied about to another. Clearly, the one who has been offended is not at fault. But he may not know what to do in the case at hand, so he seeks you out as his counselor. As a sinner himself he might contemplate sinful responses. He may suggest "getting even." But you point out that Romans 12 forbids this: vengeance belongs to God, not to man. He may suggest ignoring the other party in the future. But that raises two other problems. First, it shows no love for theone who lied. Second, it fails to resolve the problem (the lie has not been countered; the attitude of your counselee probably will tend to become resentful, and/or bitter). The first of these secondary problems is met in Galatians 6:1ff. and Luke 17:3ff., where concern for one who sins is laid upon others (even the one sinned against). The second of these secondary problems is dealt with in Ephesians 4:25ff., where attitudes are dealt with and the problem of lying is confronted. So, on the basis of these passages (and others that might be adduced), you will not allow your counselee to ignore the wrong. And so it goes. In other words, at every point you will look for the sin involved and its effects. Dealing with the effects alone is not sufficient. The root of the problem must be dealt with. So, you will advise your counselee to confront the brother who lied about him in accordance with Luke 17, Matthew 18:15 (etc.) so as to deal with the cause of the offense. The effects – what others think as the result of the lie – will also be dealt with in due course as the repentant wrongdoer goes back and confesses his lie. But the main problem is to get your counselee to do something about the liar himself – to help him to put off lying and become a truth teller. This, in turn, should have other good effects: the strengthening of the individual and his church, the cementing of a deeper relationship between your counselee and the individual concerned and the honor of God in it all. It will become very clear throughout the process that you are dealing with sin and its effects. You will not be able to excuse what has happened on any other basis. Only in the Lord Jesus Christ can you find a solution to the difficulty that sin brought into being. He, and He alone, is the answer to sin and the misery it brings.

Yes! So sin *is* the problem. Never forget it. That is the large, fundamental understanding of all problems that counselees encounter. Any lesser understanding of the counseling situation is inadequate and leads those concerned in the wrong direction. They will focus on one or another *effect* of sin rather than on its source – sin.

He's got a wrong premise. Misguided. It's both/and

Chapter 11

YOU MUST BECOME AN INTERPRETER

A person who can't interpret the Word of God properly can't counsel biblically. It is wrong to talk about being biblical and then all but ignore serious Bible study. To use the Bible in a shallow, simplistic fashion (that in many cases misinterprets what God is saying) is inexcusable. If you want to become an excellent counselor, then you must first become an excellent interpreter.

Is there really a problem here? Yes, most definitely. If you read only a small portion of the so-called "Christian" counseling literature out there you know that there's a problem. If you are still not sure, judge for yourself. Here are a few examples. One counselor, who purports to be a Christian, quoted Oscar Pfister, Freud's confidante, as saying this: "Tell me what you find in the Bible and I'll tell you what you are." He then went on to say, "The Bible is a mirror into which a person projects his own concept of himself and which in turn reflects it back." He said that was his understanding of James 1:22-24. What he did was turn the Bible into a Rorschach test.

Here's another example: "God wants us to love in ourselves the person created by Him in His image." Do you think God wants you to love the person He created in you? Why did God create you

You Must Become an Interpreter

in His image? So that you would love *Him*, not yourself! If I hand a picture of my wife to you and say, "This is my wife," what will my reaction be if you tear it to shreds, throw it on the ground, spit on it and jump all over it? Do that and you're in trouble. Why? Because the paper and the ink are so valuable? No. You're in trouble because you attacked and insulted what that paper represented – my wife. The image of God in man is important because of the One Whose image it is, not because of man, who is only the paper and the ink.

One counselor misuses Jeremiah's statement that God will not remember our sins (31:34) to support his view of the "healing of the memories" – as if God ever forgot anything! This counselor wrongly equates *not remembering* with *forgetting*. He goes so far with this unbiblical interpolation as to write "Perhaps God Himself has had some kind of healing of His memories." If that isn't misusing Scripture and insulting our God while doing so, I don't know what is. What kind of theology is this? Does he even have a legitimate doctrine of God?

In writing a book on forgiveness, a counselor wrote this: "Christ's way was the way of forgiveness even before asked. He prayed, 'Father, forgive them.' That's forgiveness, unasked, undeserved, yet freely given." But even casual exegesis reveals that there was no forgiveness granted from the cross. Jesus' statement was a *prayer* that God would forgive, not a *granting* of forgiveness to those who were crucifying Him. Did God ever answer the prayer? Yes. He did so on the Day of Pentecost, and on subsequent occasions when Peter preached. Those who by God's mercy repented and believed were the first of many answers to Jesus' prayer. But forgiveness was not granted apart from repentance and faith.

How often have you heard an explanation of Romans 8:15, 16 where we read "the Spirit witnesses *with* our spirit," as meaning that He witnesses *to* our spirits? Just a little study in any good commentary would make it clear that the Greek preposition, *sun* used there doesn't mean "to" but "together with." The Spirit, as one of two witnesses, witnesses ***together with*** our spirit that we are the sons of God. It's not the Spirit witnessing to us, but together with us.

When will be the last time that you hear someone misusing I Thessalonians 5:22? Paul urges us to avoid every appearance of evil. Almost any commentary of any merit explains that Paul isn't saying, "Avoid things that *look like* evil but aren't," but that he was saying, "Avoid genuine evil in whatever form it appears and wherever it appears."

In the light of such statements I ask, "Is it necessary to learn to interpret the Bible so that you can counsel skillfully and accurately? Isn't there much work to be done?" I'm talking about genuine, in depth study of the sort that Ezra engaged in. You must learn to discover the real meaning of every passage that you use in counseling. God is not obligated to bless your every use of His Word. He may do as He wishes, of course, but He makes no promise that He will do so. And He does not excuse you for misunderstanding or misusing that Word. Jesus thought that proper interpretation was an important matter, as we can see in His words to counselors who were leading others astray by their erroneous interpretations of the Old Testament law. He said, "You have taken away the key to the house of knowledge. You didn't go in yourselves, and you have hindered those who were entering." That's serious. Not only did they jeopardize themselves before God, but they also placed others in jeopardy by their erroneous interpretations.

Peter spelled out the severity of the problem in II Peter 3:16-18. Referring to Paul's writings, Peter said that his letters contain some things hard to understand which the untaught and unstable distort as they do also the rest of the Scriptures, to their own destruction. You, therefore, beloved, knowing this beforehand, be on your guard so that you are not carried away by the error of unprincipled men and fall from your own steadfastness.

It is dangerous, says Peter, to follow those who twist and warp the Scriptures.

The Bible is not a book to read casually like a newspaper. To understand it one must prayerfully pour his heart and soul into it, using all the effort and skills necessary to do so. God didn't make the Bible hard to understand in order to create a puzzle, but some parts are more difficult to interpret than others. Because we are so foolish, sinful, lazy and blind, it is often hard for us to pry those truths loose. A surface reading of the Bible isn't enough. We have to study it the right way.

Along these lines, I am troubled by the word *devotions*. When people speak of studying the Bible "devotionally" I really don't know what that means. I'm afraid that too often it means closing one's mind to what the passage was intended to teach while hoping that something in it may strike one in some warm, fuzzy way. This idea leads one to avoid researching what the passage means; it is the adoption of a mystical method of reading the Bible. There is nothing about a devotional use of the Bible in the Bible itself.

If, on the other hand, one *studies* his Bible devotionally, he will not use it superficially. He will bring all his acumen and skills to the practice. He will take time to understand the meaning of the passage, perhaps consulting commentaries and other books in order to do so. Only then will he accurately apply the passage to life.

In accord with this, many counselors bend and twist the Scriptures to fit ideas previously adopted from pagan systems of counseling. Predictably, when an integrationist with a Ph.D. in psychology and a Sunday School degree in Bible attempts to interpret the Bible, the Bible gets bent to fit the psychology. But, as Peter said, when the Bible gets twisted and tortured on the rack, that ends up destroying people. Scripture-twisting is to be neither encouraged nor allowed.

Pastors and elders, who know better, have an obligation to put a stop to it whenever they have in their congregations counselors who engage in such activities. If they will not change, these counselors should be disciplined.

Why do such people do this? In verse 16 Peter is clear on the point. It is because they are untaught and unstable. God puts no premium on ignorance. He wants teachers and counselors to be enlightened by His knowledge and wisdom. The first chapter of Proverbs teaches us that understanding, discernment and knowledge are part of God's will for our lives. The Bible is given to impart wisdom: "the fear of the Lord is the beginning of wisdom." Many counselors are *untaught* because they spend their time studying psychology rather than the Bible. Recently a secular book entitled *Fad Surfing* was published. Its focus is on organizations going through wave after wave of new ideas to re-engineer or reinvent their businesses so as to operate better. But after being swept along with so many different waves, managers in these organizations are becoming worn out. They are tired of unsettling their employees time and again. This same problem also applies to counselors who are getting caught in the undertow.

There was a time when Freud was in vogue. Next Rogers became the fad. Then Skinner. Next a tidal wave of varying views came flooding in. People who have promoted wave after wave of new counseling systems have never learned how to interpret the Scriptures. They are, as Peter said, **unstable**. And being unstable, they move from one view to another. Fad surfing goes on in Christian counseling circles because people are unstable. Their roots are not very deep. People, like tumbleweeds, are blown about every time the wind shifts direction. Instead of refining and deepening one's knowledge, he is forced to uproot and replant with the next psychological view that appears. To jettison one counseling system after another is not only tiring, but also is detrimental to counselors and to the church. People like this are described in II Timothy 3:7.

According to Peter, this twisting of the Scriptures is infectious. He speaks of being on guard not to be carried away by it. Some teachers simply don't know any better. Others, for nefarious purposes, will mislead people. They are "unprincipled," as Peter says. Even though they know they are not helping others, they go on pretending, practicing and propagating error. And they will fight fiercely against the truth when it opposes their duplicity.

What should you do if you want to be different? (And you should!) If possible, take a course in Bible interpretation, hermeneutics or exegesis, terms that I shall soon explain. Get some serious instruction in Bible study. You will never become a competent counselor if you are always changing counseling systems. The Word of God is stable. Counselors who plant their feet firmly upon Scripture are set for life. They will never have to scrap a system or severely retool their approach. They will learn more and more about what they have. What a difference that makes! Counselor, if you want to excel, you must become a Bible interpreter of the first water. In the next chapter, we shall enlarge on this thought, looking a bit more closely at what is involved.

Chapter 12

WHAT INTERPRETATION IS ALL ABOUT

There are three terms that are important to the proper interpretation of the Bible. You should familiarize yourself with them and what they refer to.

Hermeneutics is the first. Sometimes people jokingly ask, "Herman who?" But the joke isn't that far from the truth. The word actually comes from the name of a mythical individual, Hermes. He was supposedly the messenger and interpreter of the Greek gods. Today, however, the word has lost all of its pagan connotations. But it does continue to carry the idea of a messenger who interprets someone else's message to others.[34] Thus, today the word means simply to "explain, interpret," as it does in Luke 24:27: "Beginning with Moses, Jesus went through all the prophets and ***explained*** to them in all the Scriptures the things that concerned Himself." By explaining the Bible Jesus was engaged in hermeneutics. Today, we use the word to mean the science of biblical interpretation or explanation. It includes the theory, principles, and practices of Bible interpretation systematically set forth.

The actual practice of putting those principles into effect during Scriptural study is called *exegesis*, the second term with which you should become familiar. It is an intensive form of a

---

34 In theological use hermeneutics is relaying God's biblical message to others.

Greek word that means "to lead out." It refers to the act of leading or drawing out an author's thoughts from his writings. In exegesis, you extract these thoughts by using hermeneutical tools according to hermeneutical principles. By this effort you transfer thoughts from the Scriptures to your own heart and mind so that you are able to comprehend and ultimately explain these truths to others.

In other words, when you do exegesis properly you apply the principles of interpretation in such a way that you get out of the Bible what God put into it. You avoid pouring some of your own ideas into the mix. And you attempt to not miss anything either, thereby avoiding diluting what God intended. As we dip into God's truth exegetically, up comes life-giving water that refreshes and quenches the soul's thirst. That's exegesis – indeed that is truly studying the Bible *devotionally*!

Calvin (the first great exegete of the Scriptures) wrote, "It is the first business of an interpreter to let the author say what he does instead of attributing to him what we think he ought to say." To put it one other way, exegesis involves the use of every piece of relevant knowledge and experience and every available help to bring out the Holy Spirit's precise meanings and intentions in the writings of the book one is studying. The great failure of many counselors is the failure to heed Calvin's exhortation.

The last of the three terms is one other non-technical term that helps us understand Bible interpretation; it is the word *opening*. This word appears in Luke 24:32 and 45 along with those other terms. It means *to explain by opening*. Do you remember how Jesus said that the Pharisees had taken away the key of knowledge, locked the door and thrown the key away? They kept people from learning divine truth. They did so by failing to exegete and apply Scripture correctly. By contrast, opening is putting the key into the lock and opening the door of knowledge. It's saying, "Here's what God says in His book," then showing someone exactly how that is true.

All explaining itself ought to be opening. That is what ministering the Word in a counseling session is all about. It is showing the intent of the writer so clearly that those who listen say in their hearts, "Ah! I see what God's talking about." Opening allows counselees to *see for themselves* what God is saying in any given passage of Scripture. By the time you are through laying out the passage before him, he will find it impossible to say, "Well, that's just the counselor's idea." Instead, he will have to say, "The counselor opened that passage in such a way that I can see perfectly that what he is saying is what the Bible says. His ideas come from God." That stands in stark contrast to a superficial use of Scripture in which a counselor (literally or figuratively) hands a Bible passage to a counselee saying, "Take this three times a day with prayer." That isn't *ministering* the word. It is merely dispensing it. Ministering the Scriptures means exegeting in such a way that you have *opened* the Bible to your counselee. Then, if a counselee backs away from a biblical injunction, he is unable to say "Oh well, that's just what the counselor thinks." Instead, he knows he is rejecting God's Word to him – with all the serious consequences that such action involves.

Just as there are three key terms related to understanding Scripture, so there are three key goals in Bible interpretation that every counselor should set before himself. He ought to strive (1) to neither add nor subtract from the thoughts and intents of the Holy Spirit but (2) to reproduce them exactly in words that are fully understood (3) by the interpreter and by those he counsels. These are prerequisite to truly biblical counseling.

Why are these things important? Because of what God says a true counselor does. I have noted His words in Isaiah 40:13,14. where we are reminded that God doesn't need man to counsel His Spirit. In the course of that argument, remember, Isaiah lists the things a faithful counselor normally does – things of which God has no need: a counselor informs, directs, gives understanding and discernment, and teaches. He does these things, as Isaiah 41:28 further indicates, in order to *answer* people's questions. So if you are going to become an able biblical counselor, you must become a faithful interpreter.

There are also three important elements in the interpreting process, each of which plays a significant part. The first of these elements is the *human* element. It's your part.[35] I Corinthians 2 makes it clear that unless the Spirit of God dwells within a person, he cannot interpret the Word of God. Paul says that Scriptural truth is spiritually discerned. That means, of course, it is discerned by the illumination of the Spirit within a person.

Thus, the first requirement for faithful Bible interpretation is salvation. We cannot expect unbelievers to understand the Bible. Sure, they can read the words and understand certain aspects of the Bible on a superficial level, but to really grasp the Scriptures in a life-changing way – ? Well, they haven't got a clue! Paul puts it this way: **"Eye has not seen and ear has not heard and neither has it entered into the heart of man what God has prepared for those who love Him"** (I Corinthians 2:9). The unbeliever has eyes that read, but do not see. He has ears that listen, but do not hear. He has a heart that is stone cold to the things of God. To receive them as truth he must have that heart replaced with a heart of flesh (Ezekiel 36:26). This change takes place only when the Spirit is poured into a person's heart (Romans 5:5). Then, and then alone, does he have the capacity to understand Scripture and respond in love. So the salvation of the interpreter is the first prerequisite for Bible interpretation.

Now, think for a moment with me about discernment. Unless one comes to the Bible with the right attitude and at the right stage in his spiritual growth, he will be limited as to what he may understand and how well he understands it. There's nothing

---

35 Of course the counselee adds to the human dimension, but we are here concerned solely with the counselor.

magical about reading and understanding the Bible. Some think that if they just read a certain number of words or chapters every day at a certain hour that will make a great difference in their lives. And by the grace of God – it might! The Word might snag them at some point. But reading words is not the same thing as studying them. God places no premium on ignorance or sloth. And He doesn't work in any mystical or magical fashion. So the counselor's state of sanctification is also important.

Have you ever sat reading the newspaper, and your eye traveled down a column of print from the top to the bottom, but you suddenly realize that you haven't the faintest idea what those words were saying even though you looked at every one of them? Why was this? Because you were listening to a conversation in the other room. Unfortunately, that's just about the way many people read the Bible – even counselors! Their eyes are merely going over print. Because they don't understand, their minds soon focus on something else. They don't understand, because they don't study the passage. It is better to read one sentence with comprehension than a full chapter without it.

Perhaps, also, those who fail to interpret correctly do so because their own spiritual lives are in such a sad condition that though they are believers, they cannot understand very well. Hebrews 5 speaks about this problem. In verse 12 and 14 we read,

> *For though by this time you ought to be teachers you have need again for someone to teach you the elementary principles [rudiments] of the oracles of God; and you have come to need milk and not solid food…Solid food is for the mature, who because of practice have their senses trained to discern between good and evil.*[36]

---

36 For details about this passage and others see my *A Call for Discernment*

The writer is not speaking of people who had never attained any knowledge of the Bible. These were people who once had some understanding but, because of their deteriorating spiritual condition, had lost it. In verse 11 he mentions the reason for their deterioration: "you have become dull of hearing." The word *dull* was even used by Greek writers to describe people who were in a coma.

It is sad when Christians who have learned and known truth come to the point of near unconsciousness of it. But it's also sad that others have never grown to the kind of maturity in which they learn enough to "teach others." Like babies, they are still sucking at a bottle! Babies are cute. I have nine grandchildren and four children, so I know about babies and bottles. But an adult sitting around sucking at milk from a bottle is kind of disgusting. Since these Christians had grown unaccustomed to the Word of righteousness (they had let up on their study of the Scriptures) and had regressed to spiritual babyhood (cf. 5:13), they became dull. So if you want to interpret the Bible, you must grow spiritually. And to grow spiritually, you must *begin to interpret* the Bible. It is like the chicken and the egg. Once begun, the process is thereafter cyclical.

If you want to be able to help people by the use of the Word, you must first have that Word in your heart and mind. You can't be dull of hearing. You have to be sharp and alert and have your senses biblically trained to discern between good and evil. Integrationists (the *spermalogoi* of chapter three) are undiscerning. Otherwise they would not be integrationists. And they lack discernment precisely because they are not accurate exegetes and interpreters of Scripture.

One thing that hinders a Christian from becoming the interpreter he needs to be is his sin. Often it is the sin of laziness. Scriptural study of the sort that is necessary for biblical counseling takes time and effort. It can be exhausting. It involves commitment. So the human element is very important in the matter of biblical interpretation. Sin clouds perception, causes distortion, and may even cause a person to avoid certain portions of the Bible that deal with it. Sin in a would-be counselor's life, or the lack thereof, has everything to do with how he interprets the Word.

Some counselors will always steer around certain issues when they encounter them in the lives of counselees because they have not applied these scriptural portions to their own lives. This is just one important example of the human element in counseling: it (of course) has many other dimensions.

The second element is the *literary* element. The Bible is literature. Everywhere that Christianity has gone, it has promoted education and literacy so that people may read and understand God's Word. People have no right to say, "I'm just going to sit and listen. I don't like to study." When God was so gracious as to give you a written revelation of His will in an accessible and convenient form, you are simply ungrateful if you neglect it. Every Christian – but counselors especially – needs to spend as much time as he can studying the Bible.

Furthermore, there are language issues to consider when studying the Bible. Though the Bible is unique, nevertheless it is literature. It is inspired literature; that makes it different from every other kind of literature. The Bible is the one place where you know that everything you read is true. There are no errors. It is the pure Word of God.

But that does not mean that it is not literature. It was written in a language. It requires some notion of grammar. It necessitates some understanding of the history and social mores of the time. One must know something about the various genres of literature that are found from Genesis to Revelation. There is narrative, poetry, prophecy, parable, apocalyptic, proverb and gospel in the Bible. And each of these types of literature has its own canons of interpretation. As a student of the Word you must become familiar with the kind of literature that you are studying. How do you interpret a proverb of two lines and a narrative of two chapters? You need to learn. Each genre of literature must be treated differently.

Finally, there is the *divine* element. I have mentioned it all along. But here, let me emphasize that both inspiration and illumination come to the fore. Only the Holy Spirit can apply inerrant Scripture to people's lives so as to effect change. Sanctification comes through God's truth: "Sanctify them by Your truth; Your Word is truth" (John 17:17). What does the word "sanctify" mean? It means that Christians are more and more being set apart from sin unto righteousness. It means putting off sinful habits of thinking and acting (cf. Isaiah 55:8). It means more and more thinking God's thoughts after Him and walking in His footsteps. The Holy Spirit produced the Bible. And He does not work apart from it. It is His tool for changing His people's lives. When the Bible is studied and applied, He works through it to effect change. He gives no new revelation. All that is necessary for "life and godliness" is found in biblical promises (II Peter 1:3, 4). God gave His Word to bring about change. When counselors fail to use the Scriptures in counseling, they shut off the avenue that leads to change.

The Holy Spirit told the apostles that they didn't have to prepare beforehand what they would preach (cf. Luke 10; Luke 21). In these statements you will find four key things that the Holy Spirit promised the apostles. These four elements make the ministry of the Word in preaching or counseling effective. Let's consider the four things mentioned. God promised to give the apostles *the right thing* (the **what**), in the *right words* (the **how**), in the *right way* (with **wisdom**), at the *right time* (**in that hour**). You ought to be concerned about these four things in your ministry of the Word since they were uppermost in the work of the Spirit as He enabled the apostles to minister it.

The three elements of interpretation, then, are the human element, the literary element and the divine element. All three must come together in a fruitful blend in the counseling room. In counseling, it is not fundamentally you and the counselee who are involved: it is the Spirit and the counselee. Every counseling session ought to be a time when the Spirit and the counselee (or counselees) are brought into close proximity to one another. That is done through the proper ministry of the Word. You want the counselee to know by the way in which you minister that it is God – not you – Who is addressing Him. That is what the *opening* of the Word (previously mentioned) is all about. Counselees should recognize that every counseling session is conducted in the presence of God. Remember it is the Spirit Who changes people – by His Word. You do not. When all three elements (the human, literary and divine) are in sync, God's meaning and purpose in a passage are understood. That means that there is power present. To the extent that one or more of these are out of sync you weaken a counseling session. No wonder many sessions are ineffective.

I have sought to do four things as we have considered biblical interpretation and counseling:

1. To highlight the importance of careful biblical interpretation.
2. To call on you to become a sound interpreter.
3. To urge you to do solid interpretation before and during counseling sessions so as to open the Bible for counselees.
4. To help you to develop an exegetical conscience so that you will never knowingly misuse a passage of the Bible.

A biblical counselor deals with Scripture. It cannot be otherwise. When he does so, then, he must carefully select the passages that he uses, accurately interpret them, and rigorously apply and appropriately implement them. That is what interpretation is all about.

Chapter 13

GRACIOUS GOODNESS

> *I myself am convinced about you, my brothers, that you yourselves are full of goodness, filled with all knowledge, and competent to counsel one another.*

Romans 15:14 is an enthymeme. What is an enthymeme? The word is used in rhetoric to describe an incomplete syllogism. The syllogism consists of three lines (terms); the enthymeme contains two of the three. One is missing. Here, the complete syllogism might have looked something like this:

- People filled with all sorts of goodness and all knowledge are competent to counsel.
- You are filled with all sorts of goodness and all knowledge.
- Therefore, you are competent to counsel.

The first term, as you can see from consulting the verse, is missing. But it is taken for granted. Another syllogism is located at the beginning of the Twenty-third Psalm: ***The Lord is my Shepherd; I shall not lack.*** The missing term in the syllogism is that shepherds meet all the needs of the sheep.

So, according to the Scriptures, a very important quality in bringing about competence in counseling is **goodness**. In Romans 15:14 Paul wrote that goodness (along with knowledge) made the Roman Christians competent to counsel. What is this goodness of which Paul speaks? Well, Christians are considered good in the sight of God because of their forensic standing in Christ. Jesus' righteousness is counted, or reckoned, to the believer so that on the books all the righteous acts of Christ are attributed to him. Before the law he is considered another person; the old person is done away with. Legally, he was counted a guilty, condemned sinner. Now he stands free from all culpability, declared righteous before the bar of heaven. That is a wonderful fact and in no way is to be minimized. However, it is not his righteous standing, considered as "goodness," that is in view in Romans 15:14. Rather, it is his character.

The word *agathosune* used by Paul also occurs in Galatians 5:22 and in Ephesians 5:9, where it obviously describes not the act of justification but an aspect of the work of sanctification. In both places, it is viewed as "the fruit of…" That is to say, the *result* of something that is at work producing it. In Galatians it is the "fruit of the Spirit," and in Ephesians it is the "fruit of the light." *Agathgosune,* then, is descriptive of the new character that is being developed by the Spirit in the believer. He does this by bringing more and more light into his life.

Rather than think of the legal or forensic standing of the Christian before the heavenly court, when one reads of his "goodness" one should think of an intrinsic attitude of kindliness and mercy. It is a personal quality that is in view. The stress is on *the goodness that one shows toward others.* He is a person who by his attitudes and actions exhibits merciful, friendly, helpful attitudes and actions in his relationships to believers and unbelievers alike. When you describe him to someone, you say, "Now there is a good man!"

The quality of goodness is not native to sinners. Men are born with the opposite tendencies. They are self-centered and caught up in what they can get or do for themselves. They are not naturally prone to help or care for others. Often they are hostile, mean spirited and selfish. "Oh," you say, "I know some unbelievers who you might say possess the quality of goodness that you have described." No, what you see in them is outward action that superficially might pass for goodness. But it is outward only – like the "goodness" of the young lawyer who addressed the Lord Jesus as "Good master," and was told that there was none good but God. The "good" works of unbelievers, as described in Hebrews 6:1, actually are "dead works." That is so precisely because they stem from one who has no spiritual life. Their deeds are done for some other reason than to honor God and are motivated by some other spirit than the Spirit of God. These works are *not* the fruit of the Spirit.

And, I know that your next response is that you have seen unbelievers who do more good than Christians. Granted, they do– if you consider their deeds truly "good." But, as I have just tried to show, God accepts as good only that which is wrought in a person by His Spirit. All other works are filthy rags. They outwardly imitate the real thing. There is nothing about them that to the all-seeing eye of God is acceptable. He Who looks upon the heart knows the motivation behind them, and is not pleased with them. True works of goodness by the believer, in a given instance, may be few and far between because he has grown so little in his faith. That is why, in the eyes of those who cannot see the heart, they seem to pale by comparison with some unbeliever's "dead works." But if the Spirit dwells within a person, there will be some measure (however small) of genuine fruit, an aspect of which is *agathosune*. The goodness of which Paul wrote is gracious goodness – goodness that comes from the grace of God alone.

This disposition Paul calls goodness is a developing quality. However, some believers excel in it; they are *"full* of goodness." This description is important. Paul does not say that if one has *some* goodness, he is competent to counsel. No, he says because they are *full* of goodness this quality makes them so. What does he mean by being full of goodness?

Biblical language elsewhere is helpful. We read about those who were filled with fear, filled with joy or filled with the Spirit. In each and every case the fullness in question means that at the time it was true of a person, this characteristic dominated him. Whatever he said and did was influenced by the fact that he was terribly afraid. Fear dominated him. The same is true of joy. And, preeminently, it is true when one is filled with the Spirit (Ephesians 5:18): all he does is Spirit energized. Every aspect of his life is influenced by the Holy Spirit. The same is true of the person who is full of goodness. His life is filled with good attitudes and acts toward others. He is dominated by kindliness. When you see or talk to him, one of the things that you can't help but notice is his goodness of spirit toward others. That is what Paul is speaking about. That is the sort of person who is qualified to counsel. He is a person who has the outstanding trait of goodness. Why is that so important for counseling? Why does counseling suffer when there is so little goodness in the counselor?

A person full of goodness cares about others enough to put himself out for them. That is necessary in counseling. Biblical counseling is not a profession, to be served by cold, hard practitioners. It is the ministry of God's Word to suffering saints. They are in need of help; the "good" counselor is one who cares enough to give it to them. He is willing to invest the time and energy necessary to do so. When others might give up on a counselee, he will not; he will go the second mile. He is concerned enough to hang in there when the going gets tough. And sometimes it gets tough because of the counselor himself.

Many counselees are not very pleasant people. They are consumed by their woes and think little of others – even of the counselor who, in his goodness, seeks to help them. But a counselor who is full of goodness cares even for the unlovely, the unloving and the unlovable. He extends good will toward all, without showing favor.

There are those who resist the work of the Spirit. They would do anything, it seems, to avoid doing the biblical thing. They try to compromise, to wriggle out of God's commands, or to find some other way. The one who is full of goodness, however, knows that God's way is always the best way because it is the right way; so out of his goodness of heart, he will not allow them to do so. He will keep going back to the Scriptures as the answer to a counselee's problems.

Some difficult counselees will not merely resist the opening of the Scriptures by the counselor, they will also attack him as a means of "getting him off their backs." Actually, this hateful trait is seen in human beings of all sorts, from the president on down. Believers may retain much of their old ways. That's why they must put off the old person and replace him with the new person that they may become in Christ. But it is in this process of change that the counselor often engages counselees. They are struggling with putting off the old person and putting on the new. Often this process, for a time, takes the form of struggling *against* the change that the Spirit is producing. During that struggle the counselor is often treated badly by counselees. Yet, if he is filled with goodness, he cheerfully persists – even when some counselees are downright nasty to him.

This lack of gratitude will not move the counselor who is full of goodness from his task. That is because he does what he does first for God and then for the sake of the counselee. And he is not doing it at any point for himself (for money, for fame, or for any other self-serving reason). Goodness will lead a pastor, for instance, to approach a member of his congregation whose life seems to be falling apart with an offer of help (Galatians 5:1ff.). He will not always wait until his life has been destroyed and the person approaches him. It is difficult to do so, but because he cares, is compassionate, and has concern, he will make the effort and take the initiative. For details, see my book *Ready to Restore*, which is an exposition and application of Galatians 6:1ff.

"OK," you say. "I've got it. I understand that a counselor must be filled with goodness to become competent. But *how* does he attain to it? What must he do to become filled with goodness?"

That is a fair question to which we must devote a bit of time. As I mentioned above when referring to Galatians 5:22 and Ephesians 5:9, we read that goodness is described as the *fruit* of the Spirit and as the *fruit* of the light (which is the same thing). Fruit means the result of the work of the Spirit or light (possibly Light) in a person. Obviously, then, the One Who Himself is characterized by absolute, infinite goodness – God – must produce goodness in the counselor. Since it is not natural to a sinner, it must be the result of a *super*natural effort. God is the Source of all goodness in man. How does this come about? How does one walk in the light or walk in the Spirit?

I have already remarked on the fact that the Spirit uses His Word to sanctify (cf. John 17:17). So the fruit of the Spirit is the fruit of His illuminating truth for a believer, and enabling a believer to understand and apply the Scriptures to his life. That is how change takes place, including the change that leads to goodness of character. The more one immerses himself in Bible truth and then walks in that truth from day to day, the more the fruit of the Spirit (in all of its aspects, including goodness) grows. By coming more and more into the light through the use of the Bible, he becomes more and more like the One Who Himself is the Light. That means that more and more goodness floods into his life. After all, the One Who is supremely good is Jesus Christ. So, developing goodness is a matter of becoming more like Him.

Goodness in a counselor is contagious. A counselee, who may lack much of this quality in his own life, can by example (discipleship) recognize the fact that there is in this person something he lacks. So, for the value that it has on this level alone, goodness is essential to faithful, biblical counseling. It sets forth an example to which counselees can aspire.

Goodness is essential to biblical counseling for other reasons, but I shall mention only one more. Goodness reflects the goodness of God Himself. When a counselee sees that a counselor is full of goodness (kindness), because (rightly or wrongly) he often identifies God with what he sees in God's ministers, he has some faint, imperfect glimpse of what God's goodness toward him must be. This is what many counselees who have been through the wringer need to realize: God's fundamental attitude toward His children is one of goodness. He is like a kind and merciful Father Who cares. The counselor, in Christ's name, represents that God; and to the extent that he is able to do so, he should rightly represent the qualities of God to every counselee.

The opposite of goodness is harshness, stern attitudes, and a lack of concern or care. These negative, unbiblical qualities also (wrongly) represent God to counselees. They must be avoided. But, again, they may not simply be eliminated; they must be *replaced*. Goodness, that represents the kindness of God to His people, must replace them. There are, perhaps, nouthetic counselors who, in learning of the need to stress responsibility to God, have gone overboard in a manner that lacks essential goodness. Harshness should never dominate (fill) the life of a counselor. Instead there should always be a loving, caring sweet reasonableness about him. In short, he should be full of goodness. That is what the counselee should see from the outset and experience throughout counseling sessions. This does not mean that he should lessen his stress upon responsible action before God; it means that the way in which he does so accords always with goodness of heart, attitude and action.

Chapter 14

WORTHY WORKMEN IN THE WORD

When I wrote about my local auto-mechanic who repairs (not merely replaces parts), who can diagnose and remedy problems speedily, and whose prices are honest and fair, I was speaking of craftsmanship. But perhaps you'd prefer a different example of what I'm trying to convey. Would you settle for an upholsterer who refuses to recover a piece of furniture if it needs repairs as well? He has been known to almost completely rebuild a sofa before recovering it so that in the end it is superior to its original condition. That too is craftsmanship!

Craftsmanship is what Paul referred to in II Timothy 15: "**Do your best to present yourself to God tried and true, a workman who won't be ashamed, cutting the Word of truth with accuracy.**" The counselor, like the preacher, is a **Workman in the Word**. That is a wonderful description of those who handle God's holy Word. If a nouthetic counselor would care to characterize the work that he does, he could do no better than to call himself such. Not only does it accurately describe his activities, but it also places before him the great challenge of his ministry – to be a craftsman in the way in which he works with (ministers) the Word of truth. Moreover, it is a title that, at all times, sets before him the meaning and purpose of what he does when he counsels. Possibly the title doesn't strike you with the same delight and challenge as it does for me, but I ask you not to dismiss it too readily. Think about it for a while.

At any rate, in Paul's words a number of factors surface (there may be more, but these are obvious):

1. The accurate handling of the Scriptures, about which I have already written extensively in this book. To those words I shall add but a little, emphasizing the verse under consideration.
2. The Word of God is called the Word of truth.
3. The possibility of shame when one presents himself before God someday.
4. The exhortation to do one's best; to become a craftsman who someday will be able to rejoice in God's proclamation "well done."

Let us begin, then, with the first of these four factors — the accurate handling of God's Word. In the King James version the passage reads "rightly dividing." However, the original term does not refer to the dividing up of the Bible into dispensations or anything else. The idea behind it is "making an accurate, precise, or true cut." I have translated it in its stark, literal simplicity, **cutting the Word of truth with accuracy**. Since Paul uses the figure of a *workman* who cuts the Word, it seems clear that he is referring to the idea of the craftsmanship of a carpenter or a stone mason who must make an accurate fit — measure twice, cut once. As I wrote in my exposition of this passage in *The Christian Counselor's Commentary* on I and II Timothy, your task is to use the Scriptures in a mature and helpful manner.

> To that end, you should do all you can to **present yourself to God tried and true, a workman who won't be ashamed, cutting the Word of truth with accuracy**.

That means that as a workman, sawing or chipping and

fitting pieces of lumber or stone, he must be sure that his cuts are straight. So too must the biblical workman in the Word cut and fit passages to people in various circumstances with similar accuracy. Otherwise, he will someday be ashamed when the Lord speaks to him about how he has handled His Word. Your ministry should be characterized by accurate and effective use of the Bible. Surely you must learn how to find the right biblical board or stone to fit the counseling situation and, how to explain and apply it to those involved, never misusing one verse. That should be your goal. To be able to do so, you must spend much more time doing biblical interpretation than the time you spend reading books about counseling – including those in this series (although the purpose of these commentaries is to return the counselor's focus to the Bible).

We shall consider next the Scriptures as *the Word of truth*. Paul doesn't say that the Bible is true; rather, he calls it the Word of truth. While the truth of what is written in its sixty-six books is clearly affirmed by that phrase, it says more. Paul is making it clear to Timothy and everyone who ministers, that the Word with which he works is the one and only Source of truth that God has provided for mankind. All other sources of information are flawed because of the sin of those who provide them. Other sources may more-or-less contain truth; but at the same time, they contain error. But none of them can be rightly called the Word of truth. The Bible *is* truth (cf. John 17:17) and is, therefore, *the one place* to turn to access truth about God, the universe, man and salvation.[37]

That Paul so designates the Scriptures is important. He wants the workman in the Word to treat it with the utmost respect and care. What he is working with is far more precious than an

---

[37] General revelation is suppressed by sinners. It may be understood only through the Bible.

expensive automobile or piece of furniture. The Psalmist says that it is more valuable than much fine gold. Indeed, there is no adequate comparison. After all, it is the very word of the living God inscripturated. So Paul is calling for exquisite care in how one ministers that Word. It is not to be treated lightly; it is the most valuable possession that exists on earth. A workman who handles God's Word, then, must be a craftsman of the highest order. Valuable items should not be placed in the hands of incompetent or careless workers. There is no place for sloppy or slipshod work. One must not cut carelessly or do inferior work. Nouthetic counselors are, in this verse, called to be ***committed to craftsmanship***.

Now, growing out of this understanding of the worth of the Word is a third factor: the possibility of shame associated with the kind of work one has done as a minister of the Word. Some day, Paul makes clear, we shall all stand before the judgment seat of God (Romans 14:10) when "each of us will give an account of himself before God" (v. 12; cf. also II Corinthians 5:10). The question before us all is what sort of evaluation of our work will God give on that day? A workman who has done inferior work when he was able to do better will be sorry that he did not live up to the potential that he had in Christ. Surely all of us will regret the wasted time that was spent on other matters when we might have been improving our ability to cut the Word more accurately. As you are endeavoring to become a worthy workman, keep in mind that you will some day appear before God's presence to answer for the sort of job you did here.

There are workmen in the Word who scar or ruin the product that they turn out because of their carelessness and lack of concern. There are others who think that they can do things a better way than God's plans directed, who will be shown that it was their task to follow the heavenly blueprint (not to go some other way devised by them or someone else). Paul even speaks of the builder who seeks to build structures composed of "wood, hay and stubble" on the one foundation that the apostles laid (Christ). At the judgment seat of God, he says, such structures will not withstand the fires of judgment and will be burned up. The workman, because he is saved, will escape. But he will be *"saved so as by fire."* That is to say, he will get out of the structure alive, but he will not be able to take much, if anything, with him (cf. I Corinthians 3:10-15). It is a decided tragedy to have worked in vain!

Yet, one fears there will be many who, if they do not heed this warning of the apostle, will find that in presenting themselves before God they will be tried, but found not true. They will be ashamed of the careless or slipshod or presumptuous work they did in handling the Word of truth. There will be others, we cannot help thinking, who neglected the Word altogether in favor of various psychological interests. II Timothy 2:15 is a strong warning to those who are willing to settle for something less or something other than excellence in biblical counseling.

Last, we come to the exhortation to "do one's best" to be true to God in ministering the Word. Not everyone can do the same; some will excel, others will only do well. There are ten talent persons and there are five talent persons. But there will also be one talent people who do nothing to double what the Lord gave them. Some will produce a hundredfold, some sixty, and some thirty (Matthew 13:8). How much one produces will vary. How well he does so will also vary. But each can do his best – he can live up to his potential. There is no excuse for anyone to be lackadaisical about the matter. God's Name and the welfare of His church are both at stake. I have met "counselors" who think that they have arrived. They suppose that there is little more for them to learn. They may have capsulized the whole of Scripture into some small compass of a few principles or a limited number of verses, thinking that they can handle every case that they undertake with these meager resources. They are wrong. All of the Word was given for some purpose; all is necessary to meet some problem or other. No one can master the Bible in this life. Its study, and the acquisition of its truth, is a lifetime task. Poorly informing counselees, misinterpreting the Scriptures to them, misapplying truth, and a host of other failings result in counseling that is unacceptable. The most serious thing is that such counseling misrepresents God to His people.

Clearly, then, God expects workmen in the Word to commit themselves to craftsmanship. Men may settle for less – sometimes far less – but God doesn't.

Chapter 15

ENRICHED BY THE WORD WITHIN

We come to a vital matter, hinted at before but never adequately unfolded. I refer to the matter mentioned by the apostle Paul in Colossians 3:16a: *"Let the Word of Christ dwell in you richly, as you teach and counsel yourselves as wisely as possible."* This exhortation is of extreme importance to the nouthetic counselor. It is a call to gain such internal wealth in Christ's Word that one is able to "counsel wisely." But just what does that mean, practically speaking?

There are several aspects to the exhortation:

1. A call to let Christ's Word dwell within;
2. A call for a wealth of the Word dwelling within;
3. A call for the wisdom adequate to counsel God's people;
4. A recognition that counseling is done by and for the members of the church.

These four elements are all of importance to those who strive for excellence in biblical counseling.

The call to "let Christ's Word dwell within," itself consists of three elements: The word "let," the designation "Christ's" Word, and the idea of that Word "dwelling within." What does Paul mean by telling us to *Let* the Word dwell within? It would seem that the Spirit is more than willing to fill one with the Word of Christ unless a person gets in the way, thus hindering His work. There are many ways in which one may "grieve or quench the Spirit" (Ephesians 4:30; I Thessalonians 5:19). It would seem that the Spirit is always eager to do His work within the believer, but that the rate of progress rarely, if ever, equals His eagerness to bring it about. If only counselors were as willing to have change as the Spirit is willing to produce it, there would be many more superior workmen in the Word. At any rate, it seems very clear that any defect in the counselor is his responsibility alone – the Spirit may not be faulted. We have seen, for instance, that the requisite goodness a counselor needs to counsel effectively is the fruit of the Spirit. So where that fruit is absent, or at least slow in coming, it is due to the counselor's failing in his pursuit of fruit.[38]

The next item to consider is the expression "Christ's Word," a phrase that is unique to this verse. While its equivalent may be found in such expressions as "His Word" and "the Lord's Word," there is an interesting emphasis found here. Clearly what the Spirit is concerned to enrich us with is Jesus' Word (or as the exact expression puts it "the Messiah's Word"). All of Scripture, in a very real sense, is Christ's Word; but the emphasis here (what the counselor must have dwelling within) is on the truth that Jesus taught while here on the earth (now found in the Gospels) and from heaven through His apostles (cf. Acts 1:1, where the passage in the original implies that Jesus only *began* to teach while on the earth and that He continued to do so after the ascension through His Spirit inspiring the words of the apostles. Cf. also John 16:12, 13). The primary information a Christian counselor will need in counseling others will be found in the New Testament. So, while not neglecting the Old Testament, one must first and foremost

---

[38] See more on this pursuit in my book *A Theology of Christian Counseling: More Than Redemption* (Grand Rapids: Zondervan Publishing House, 1979).

devour the New. It is there that he will find (in the narrow sense) the words of Christ. That direction is important for those who are beginning to study the Scriptures.[39]

The exhortation includes the idea of this Word of Christ *dwelling within*. That means at least two things. It indicates that the counselor has a knowledge of the Word that he carries with him as portable truth. He does not always have to turn to his Bible while counseling. He is able to quote passages from memory.[40] While every counselor must memorize certain frequently used verses, it will not be possible to memorize all of them he might need in counseling. Rather than give up because of the enormity of the task or spend all of his time in memorization (rather than interpretation, etc.), it would be wise to learn the gist of passages and their book and chapter location, so that when needed in counseling they can be readily found. One reason for the marginal subject notations in *The Christian Counselor's New Testament* is to aid in this effort.

But there is a second thrust to the words "dwell within." That which *dwells* is *at ho*me there. It is not tenting (a word in the Bible that means something is temporary), but dwelling – that is, the Word settled, or rooted. In other words, the truth that one has at his command when counseling has first taken up lodging in the life of the counselor. He is not merely mouthing words; he is talking from personal experience. The Bible has become a part of his inner life (where it counts, because there the Spirit is at work using it to transform him into the stature of Christ). He is no hypocrite. The Word of Christ is not foreign to him; it is clearly a part of his own

---

39 Of course, the study of the New will often require a knowledge of the Old. In studying the Old Testament in order to understand the New one will find that he is learning both. But he will approach the Old Testament as a Christian who stands on this side of the cross, not as a person still looking for a Messiah. In that way he will learn the Word of the *Christ*.

40 Often it is wise to read a passage (even if you know it from memory) if the counselee might doubt that you are quoting accurately.

beliefs, and it influences his walk before God. We come now to the idea of the wealth of this Word. It is said to dwell *richly* within. When one possesses riches, he is able to share much wealth with others. He is not so dependent on the little that he owns that he fears to give up any for the sake of another. He has wealth to spread around – if he will. What is a few thousand here and there to a billionaire? The counselor is to be like a billionaire. Indeed, if he has the Word of Christ dwelling richly within, he is richer than a billionaire who doesn't! He has more than enough of the Word to expend on every counseling situation.

Paul means that to counsel, one must have a wealth of Scripture at his disposal at all times. A preacher knows what he'll talk about on Sunday (we hope). The counselor only has the vaguest idea of what he must face and where the case will go. Therefore, he will often find himself traversing territory that he never thought he would. Yet, even in that new and challenging territory, he should not be at a loss. His wealth of knowledge of the Word ought to be able to stand him in good stead no matter where he may travel in counseling sessions. He should never be lost, wherever he goes. To gain that sort of knowledge one must spend much time studying the Scriptures. He cannot be satisfied with a few principles that relate to a few problems. He must become acquainted with as much of the Bible as he can. The question is, "How much Scriptural wealth do you possess?" Take inventory. Tot up the amounts. Cover all sorts of subjects and determine how much you know about each of them.[41]

Third, there is the need to counsel *wisely*. The biblical idea of wisdom is *the practical use of biblical principles*. Wisdom goes beyond the intellectual knowledge of what is taught in the Bible. It reaches to the wise *use* of that teaching as it is applied to given

---

41 In the back of the *Christian Counselor's New Testament* there is a list of topics and relevant Scripture verses that may be useful in making a beginning at this effort.

situations. *How* one counsels is a matter of wisdom. *When* he says *what* can be crucial. That is why wisdom is needed in counseling. A command to flee fornication is clear. What, in a given case, is required to fulfill that command may differ from what is required in another. One should not use a canned and refrigerated approach. Often a command is encountered in the Bible, but no implementation is affixed to it. The counselor must wisely guide the counselee to the very best way in which to obey the command. That requires wisdom. Much of that will be gained through study. But much will also be gained as the counselor implements truth in his own life. And, in addition, wisdom grows as one uses the Word in counseling. A person who does not counsel regularly will not rapidly grow in this sort of wisdom. He must be at the work of using the Word over and over again in varied circumstances.

Last, Paul speaks of "counseling *yourselves*." The picture that this conveys is of believers counseling one another. It is something Paul assumes will take place. Notice, he doesn't send young couples who are having marital problems down the street to some pagan counselor. Can you even imagine Paul doing such a thing? He is clear about the fact that it is believers who must counsel believers (cf. Galatians 6:1).[42] There is too much irresponsibility in this matter in Christianity today. There are pastors who regularly farm out the counseling that they should be undertaking to a psychologist or psychiatrist. This will not do. If Paul speaks of all believers coming to the place where they can counsel (as this passage seems to indicate), then surely the pastors and the elders of a church must be able to. It is time for the church to awaken to the fact that a massive selling job has been done. Pastors and seminary professors have been sold on the idea that they are unable to help people beyond dealing with a psychic scratch. All the "deep" problems, they are assured, must be farmed out to "professionals." Let me ask you, pastor, which is

---

[42] Here he speaks of those "who have the Spirit" helping. All believers have the Spirit.

deeper, the systems of Freud or Rogers or Maslow (or some other unbeliever) which merely rearrange the furniture on the porch, or that of the Scriptures activated in the heart of the counselee so as to change him within? Who really works at a deep level? Who can change a person's heart, from which, Jesus said, all his trouble stems (cf. Matthew 15:19)? How futile it is to send people to counselors who, themselves, haven't the faintest idea about how to live so as to please God!

There seems to be no question, then, about the importance of the Word of Christ dwelling richly within. Counselors simply cannot do without this. Take it to heart if you would become a craftsman who works well with the Word.

Chapter 16

TEST YOURSELF, COUNSELOR

The following twenty brief summaries of counseling cases present a sampling of the sorts of problems commonly faced by biblical counselors. They are set forth here for you to test your competency as a nouthetic counselor. Most are fairly simple; others a bit more difficult. Read through each situation, asking yourself such questions as:

- "What do I think is wrong?
- Are there unmentioned, complicating problems?
- What relevant Scripture passages immediately come to mind?
- How would I go about dealing with the problem?
- What would I do first?"

I have included white space following each case. Use this to sketch your answers in pencil. From time to time, as your knowledge and ability to counsel grow, revisit each case and, if necessary, make revisions or additions to what you have previously written.

CASE 1: A husband says that he is attracted to a woman at his work. He claims that he has so far resisted her obvious advances. But he is growing weaker and thinks that he will be unable to control his desires much longer. His wife is furious at his revelation.

CASE 2: The wife of a preacher claims that her husband has little time for her. "He is wedded to his church," she says. He counters, "If I don't devote myself to the work, the church will fail, I'll be out of a job and I won't be able to support her and the children. She could sacrifice a little. She's unreasonable!"

CASE 3: You have been counseling some members of your congregation who are at odds over a business transaction that recently took place. "He lied and cheated," John says. "I did not," is Barney's response. He continues: "John misunderstood what I said or took something for granted that I didn't say. I never promised anything like what he claims."

CASE 4: Mary tells you that she has a fear of bridges. Even when she thinks of going across one, she freezes up and almost panics. She says that she has attempted to overcome this fear which has severely debilitated her, but every time she sets out to drive over a bridge she has a panic attack. She knows this is wrong for a Christian, but doesn't know what to do about the problem.

CASE 5: Bill recently told his wife Jill that he is going to divorce her. He says that there is no other woman and that it is not because Jill is a bad wife. He simply made a mistake in getting married. "I really wasn't ready for it," he explains, "I want my freedom again."

CASE 6: Tom and Flo sit before you crestfallen. They have just told you that Roger, their seventeen-year-old son, has been "busted" for selling drugs. "Where do we go from here?" is their question. What will be your response to this question? Incidentally, Roger is also a member of your congregation.

CASE 7: A sharp fifteen-year-old member of your church wants help in determining what he should do with his life. "I need to decide soon," he says. "I don't want to waste time and money just 'going to college,' like so many guys do. When I go I want everything I do to count for the future." How will you help him?

CASE 8: Betty has hit her husband over the head with a colander in their most recent argument which ended in a fist fight. It was only because you inquired about Fred's multiple facial bruises that you uncovered this pattern which, they say, has been going on for years. What will you do to help them?

CASE 9: Randy has just lost another job – his fourth this year so far. He says, "I don't know why I keep saying and doing foolish things. I know I shouldn't have cursed the boss and slammed the door as I walked out, but he was unreasonable." How can you help him?

CASE 10: "My bags are packed, and I'm going home to my parents *today* unless you can do something about Phil. I've had it! I won't live with him under these conditions a day longer!" Phil, who doesn't want her to leave says, "Pastor, I don't even know what her problem, is. All of a sudden she ups and goes. What will I do?" What should they do?

CASE 11: "She won't have sex with me any more! Do you know what that's like, pastor? I don't know what I will do? Can you help?" In response to Bob's statement you ask Phyllis if this is accurate. She confirms it adding, "Well, I don't get anything out of it, so why should I submit to his animal lusts?" How will you respond?

CASE 12: "I'm simply not going again. Every time I do, I end up getting hurt and go home crying." Penny is referring to a recent trip to her mother-in-law's home. Harry says, "But all that Mother did was comment about how stringy our daughter's hair is. And, you know, she was right about that!" Penny cuts in: "See, he takes up for her. He doesn't think I am a fit mother any more than she does." How will you take on this one? Incidentally, the mother-in-law lives three blocks away from them.

CASE 13: "Ever since he heard about President Clinton's affair with Monica Lewinsky he wants oral sex. I don't think that it is right, and it is repulsive to me. What do you think, Pastor?"

CASE 14: "Our kids are a hopeless mess. They won't obey, and she refuses to do anything about it. As a matter of fact, when I try to discipline them, Alice countermands my efforts and undermines my discipline. I can't be there all day the way she can, so she has the greater influence over them. It isn't right!" Mona replies, "I believe in discipline, but John's discipline is arbitrary and unreasonable. To boot, he is harsh with the children. So I simply try to temper his actions with mercy."

CASE 15: "I seriously doubt that Jesus rose from the dead. I've been reading some books that seem to have very strong counter arguments to the biblical story. Why do you believe in the resurrection, Pastor?"

CASE 16: "Pastor, there's something missing in my Christian life. I just don't seem to be making progress spiritually. What do you think is wrong?"

CASE 17: "It's her fault that we don't get along. We argue and fight all the time. If she'd only respect me, things would be different!"

"Respect him? Humph! All he does is think about himself."

"See? See how she treats me?"

"How do you respect a man who whines like that?"

CASE 18: "I just came to ask you the name of a good Christian psychologist you could recommend. My sister and husband need help. Their marriage is on the rocks."

CASE 19: "Pastor, I've been hearing and seeing things that people say aren't real. What's happening to me? Am I going crazy?" Where would you begin in seeking to help this person?

CASE 20: "I'm for putting our kids in Christian school this year. My husband thinks that I should homeschool them. I'm not sure that I want to be tied down that way every day. Why should we be so different from all of our friends, anyway?"

CPSIA information can be obtained
at www.ICGtesting.com
Printed in the USA
LVHW020829050222
710245LV00009B/182